About Skill Builders Fractions, Decimals, and Percents Level 2

by R. B. Snow and Clareen Arnold

Welcome to Rainbow Bridge Publishing's Skill Builders series. This series is designed to make learning fun and rewarding.

Fractions, Decimals, and Percents helps students expand on beginning concepts and reinforce and develop math skills. Each Skill Builders volume is grade-level appropriate, with clear examples and instructions to guide the lesson. In accordance with NCTM standards, exercises in this book cover a variety of math skills, including simplifying and renaming fractions and mixed numbers; solving equations with fractions; converting fractions and decimals; standard operations with decimals; ratios; percentages; sale and discount prices; and much more.

A critical thinking section includes exercises to develop higher-order thinking skills.

Learning is more effective when approached with an element of fun and enthusiasm. That's why the Skill Builders combine entertaining and academically sound exercises with engaging themes to make reviewing basic skills fun and effective, for both you and your budding scholars.

Table of Contents

Writing Fractions

You can represent fractions on a number line. If an interval of length 0-1 is divided into 6 equal pieces, the length of any one of the pieces represents $\frac{1}{6}$.

Remember:

$$\frac{5}{6} = \frac{\text{numerator}}{\text{denominator}}$$

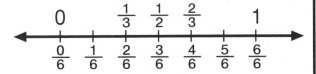

The **numerator** is the number of parts or groups represented.

The **denominator** is the total number of parts or groups.

Write each missing fraction on the number lines.

1.

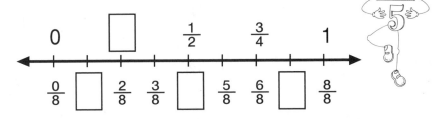

2.

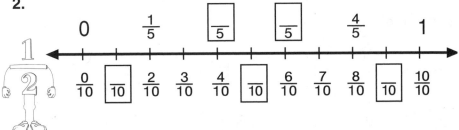

3.

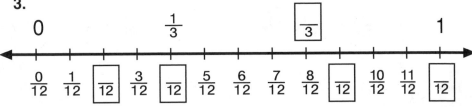

RB-904002

Equivalent Fractions

If a numerator and a denominator are each multiplied or divided by the same number, then the new fraction represents the same number.	**Example:**	$\dfrac{4}{6} = \dfrac{4 \times 2}{6 \times 2} = \dfrac{8}{12}$
		$\dfrac{4}{6} = \dfrac{4 \times 3}{6 \times 3} = \dfrac{12}{18}$
		$\dfrac{4}{6} = \dfrac{4 \div 2}{6 \div 2} = \dfrac{2}{3}$

So, $\frac{4}{6}$, $\frac{8}{12}$, $\frac{12}{18}$, and $\frac{2}{3}$ are all equivalent fractions.

For each fraction, write two equivalent fractions.

1. $\dfrac{2}{4}$ $\qquad\qquad$ $\dfrac{2}{12}$ $\qquad\qquad$ $\dfrac{8}{14}$

2. $\dfrac{10}{24}$ $\qquad\qquad$ $\dfrac{4}{9}$ $\qquad\qquad$ $\dfrac{10}{20}$

3. $\dfrac{2}{16}$ $\qquad\qquad$ $\dfrac{10}{12}$ $\qquad\qquad$ $\dfrac{8}{9}$

4. $\dfrac{3}{24}$ $\qquad\qquad$ $\dfrac{3}{10}$ $\qquad\qquad$ $\dfrac{7}{18}$

Write an equivalent fraction.

5. $\dfrac{1}{11} = \dfrac{}{33}$ $\qquad\qquad$ $\dfrac{1}{20} = \dfrac{4}{}$

6. $\dfrac{3}{15} = \dfrac{}{45}$ $\qquad\qquad$ $\dfrac{12}{20} = \dfrac{36}{}$

7. $\dfrac{3}{18} = \dfrac{}{36}$ $\qquad\qquad$ $\dfrac{12}{18} = \dfrac{}{54}$

8. $\dfrac{7}{11} = \dfrac{42}{}$ $\qquad\qquad$ $\dfrac{4}{10} = \dfrac{}{50}$

4

Example: List the factors of 12 and 18. Circle the common factors. Write the **greatest common factor (GCF)**.

Factors of 12: (1)(2)(3) 4,(6) 12
Factors of 18: (1)(2)(3)(6) 9, 18
Common Factors: (1)(2)(3)(6)   **GCF = 6**

A **factor** is a number that another number can be divided by evenly.

List the factors of each pair of numbers. Circle the common factors. Find the greatest common factor (GCF).

1.   7:

      21:

      GCF:_____

      3:

      12:

      GCF:_____

2.   20:

      32:

      GCF:_____

      6:

      24:

      GCF:_____

3.   12:

      44:

      GCF:_____

      24:

      36:

      GCF:_____

4.   9:

      18:

      GCF:_____

      18:

      30:

      GCF:_____

5.   14:

      35:

      GCF:_____

      15:

      35:

      GCF:_____

     RB-904002

Simplest Form

Example: Write the fraction $\frac{42}{56}$ in simplest form.

Step 1
Find the GCF of the numerator and denominator.
42: ①②3, 6,⑦⑭ 21, 42
56: ①②4,⑦8, ⑭ 28, 56
GCF = 14

Step 2
Divide the numerator and denominator by their GCF.

$$\frac{42}{56} \div \frac{14}{14} = \frac{3}{4}$$

Write each fraction in simplest form. Circle your answer.
If a fraction is already in simplest form, just write the fraction.

1. $\frac{8}{14}$ $\frac{2}{15}$ $\frac{28}{30}$ $\frac{5}{20}$

2. $\frac{15}{22}$ $\frac{35}{50}$ $\frac{10}{20}$ $\frac{22}{32}$

3. $\frac{18}{90}$ $\frac{75}{80}$ $\frac{30}{50}$ $\frac{20}{100}$

4. $\frac{25}{75}$ $\frac{60}{200}$ $\frac{4}{30}$ $\frac{26}{28}$

www.summerbridgeactivities.com   © Rainbow Bridge Publishing

Least Common Multiple

The **least common multiple (LCM)** is the smallest number that is a multiple of two or more numbers.

Example: Find the LCM of 6 and 8.
- List some multiples of 6 and 8.
- Circle the common multiples.
- Write the least common multiple.

Multiples of 6:
  6, 12, 18, ⓐ24, 30, 36, 42, ⓐ48
Multiples of 8:
  8, 16, ⓐ24, 32, 40, ⓐ48

LCM = 24

Find the least common multiple (LCM) of each set of numbers.

1.   2:

  5:

  LCM:_____

  5:

  7:

  LCM:_____

2.   2:

  3:

  5:

  LCM:_____

  3:

  6:

  9:

  LCM:_____

3.   6:

  5:

  15:

  LCM:_____

  4:

  9:

  18:

  LCM:_____

4.   8:

  10:

  20:

  LCM:_____

  10:

  15:

  30:

  LCM:_____

RB-904002

Two fractions have a common denominator if their denominators are the same. The **lowest common denominator** **(LCD)** of two fractions is the least common multiple of their denominators.

Step 1
Find the LCD of the two fractions.

$$\frac{5}{8} \text{ and } \frac{7}{12}$$

8: 8, 16, ㉔
12: 12, ㉔

LCD = 24

Step 2
Write equivalent fractions with the common denominator of 24.

$$\frac{5}{8} = \frac{}{24}$$
$$\frac{5}{8} = \frac{5}{8} \times \frac{3}{3} = \frac{15}{24}$$
$$\frac{7}{12} = \frac{}{24}$$
$$\frac{7}{12} = \frac{7}{12} \times \frac{2}{2} = \frac{14}{24}$$

Write equivalent fractions with the LCD.

1. $\frac{5}{6}$ and $\frac{2}{5}$ 　　　　　 $\frac{4}{5}$ and $\frac{3}{9}$

2. $\frac{3}{5}$ and $\frac{5}{6}$ 　　　　　 $\frac{1}{18}$ and $\frac{1}{9}$

3. $\frac{4}{5}$ and $\frac{6}{20}$ 　　　　　 $\frac{1}{4}$ and $\frac{3}{18}$

4. $\frac{3}{7}$ and $\frac{3}{8}$ 　　　　　 $\frac{1}{2}$ and $\frac{4}{11}$

Comparing and Ordering

To compare fractions, you need common denominators.

Example: Compare $\frac{5}{7}$ and $\frac{7}{9}$.

Step 1 Find the LCD.	**Step 2** Write equivalent fractions with the LCD.	**Step 3** Compare numerators.
7: 7, 14, 21, 28, 35, 42, 49, 56, ⑥③	$\frac{5}{7} = \frac{5}{7} \times \frac{9}{9} = \frac{45}{63}$	$\frac{45}{63} < \frac{49}{63}$
9: 9, 18, 27, 36, 45, 54, ⑥③	$\frac{7}{9} = \frac{7}{9} \times \frac{7}{7} = \frac{49}{63}$	
LCD = 63		

Compare. Write >, <, or = in the $\bigcirc$ in each problem.

1. $\frac{2}{6} \bigcirc \frac{3}{8}$ $\qquad$ $\frac{3}{5} \bigcirc \frac{8}{15}$ $\qquad$ $\frac{3}{4} \bigcirc \frac{1}{2}$

2. $\frac{1}{3} \bigcirc \frac{3}{8}$ $\qquad$ $\frac{2}{3} \bigcirc \frac{4}{5}$ $\qquad$ $\frac{3}{8} \bigcirc \frac{3}{16}$

3. $\frac{2}{7} \bigcirc \frac{1}{3}$ $\qquad$ $\frac{5}{9} \bigcirc \frac{4}{8}$ $\qquad$ $\frac{2}{9} \bigcirc \frac{1}{3}$

Order from least to greatest.

4. $\frac{5}{12}, \frac{4}{7}, \frac{3}{8}$ $\qquad\qquad$ $\frac{9}{16}, \frac{3}{4}, \frac{5}{18}$

We have less in common...

...than these numbers!

5. $\frac{3}{4}, \frac{5}{7}, \frac{9}{14}$ $\qquad\qquad$ $\frac{4}{5}, \frac{17}{20}, \frac{3}{4}$

 RB-904002

Problem Solving

Solve each problem.
Write answers in simplest terms.

1. A literary magazine has 16 pages; $5\frac{1}{2}$ pages are short stories, and $6\frac{1}{2}$ pages are poems. How many pages are not short stories or poems?

2. Tom walked $\frac{1}{4}$ of a mile, then he started running. In all, he walked and ran $\frac{3}{4}$ miles. How far did he run?

3. James lives $\frac{7}{10}$ of a mile from school. Billy lives $\frac{4}{10}$ of a mile from school. Who lives closer? By how much?

4. Michele made a book from cardboard for her project. The cover was $13\frac{1}{2}$ inches long and $9\frac{3}{4}$ inches wide. How much longer was the cover than it was wide?

5. Grayson spent his first week of school doing $4\frac{3}{4}$ hours of homework. His sister Denise spent $6\frac{1}{2}$ hours doing her homework. How much longer did Denise spend doing homework than Grayson?

6. Jennifer wants to buy some ribbon to make bookmarks. She wants to make one bookmark $6\frac{1}{8}$ inches long and the other $9\frac{13}{16}$ inches long. How much ribbon should she buy?

www.summerbridgeactivities.com   © Rainbow Bridge Publishing

Problem Solving:
Fractions in a Bar Graph

The Chamber of Commerce surveyed tourists to see what activities they participated in while visiting the capital city. The graph shows the fraction of all tourists who took part in each activity.

Solve using the graph. Write all fractions in simplest form.

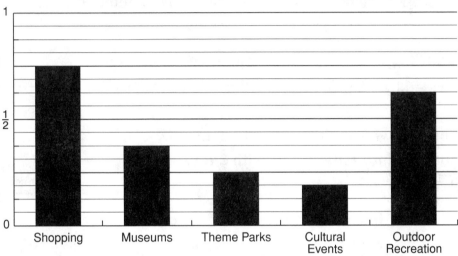

1. Which activities were chosen by fewer than $\frac{1}{2}$ of the tourists?

2. What fraction of tourists participated in the second most popular activity?

3. In what two activities combined did less than half of the tourists participate?

4. In which activity did $\frac{1}{4}$ of the tourists participate?

5. What fraction of the tourists enjoyed outdoor recreation?

        RB-904002

Writing Mixed Numbers

A **mixed number** is made up of a whole number and a fraction.

whole number → $3\frac{1}{2}$ ← fraction

An **improper fraction** has a numerator that is greater than or equal to the denominator.

Improper fraction → $\frac{7}{2} = 3\frac{1}{2}$ ← mixed number

Example:

Write $\frac{10}{4}$ as a mixed number. The fraction bar stands for "divided by." So, $\frac{10}{4}$ means "10 divided by 4."

Think: How many times does 4 go into 10?

Four goes into ten **2 times, with 2 remaining.**

So, $\frac{10}{4} = 2\frac{2}{4} = 2\frac{1}{2}$

$$
\begin{array}{r}
2 \\
4{\overline{\smash{\big)}\,10}} \\
\underline{-8} \\
2
\end{array}
$$

2 ← number of wholes

2 ← number of fourths remaining

Write each fraction as a whole number or a mixed number.

1. $\frac{4}{3}$ $\frac{5}{2}$ $\frac{25}{5}$ $\frac{17}{12}$

2. $\frac{10}{3}$ $\frac{81}{9}$ $\frac{43}{13}$ $\frac{31}{5}$

3. $\frac{28}{3}$ $\frac{51}{8}$ $\frac{60}{9}$ $\frac{60}{12}$

4. $\frac{55}{11}$ $\frac{17}{2}$ $\frac{76}{10}$ $\frac{27}{5}$

Writing Improper Fractions

Write $5\frac{2}{5}$ as an improper fraction.

$5 \times 5 = 25$

$25 + 2 = 27$

$5\frac{2}{5} = \frac{27}{5}$

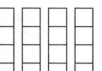

$\frac{25}{5} + \frac{2}{5} = \frac{27}{5}$

Write each mixed number as a **reduced** improper fraction.

1. $8\frac{2}{3}$ $\qquad$ $5\frac{2}{5}$ $\qquad$ $2\frac{9}{18}$

2. $6\frac{3}{4}$ $\qquad$ $3\frac{3}{7}$ $\qquad$ $10\frac{2}{3}$

3. $10\frac{2}{5}$ $\qquad$ $11\frac{1}{11}$ $\qquad$ $1\frac{7}{16}$

Rename 3 as a fraction with a denominator of 5.

$3 = \overline{5}$

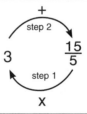

Multiply the 3 and the 5 to find the numerator.

Write each mixed number as a **reduced** improper fraction.

4. $1 = \overline{5}$ $\qquad$ $1 = \overline{12}$ $\qquad$ $4 = \overline{2}$

5. $8 = \overline{3}$ $\qquad$ $10 = \overline{3}$ $\qquad$ $12 = \overline{5}$

6. $18 = \overline{3}$ $\qquad$ $11 = \overline{5}$ $\qquad$ $13 = \overline{2}$

RB-904002

To add or subtract fractions that have the same denominator:

Step 1	Step 2	Step 3
Add or subtract the numerators to find the numerator of the answer.	Write the denominator of the fractions as the denominator of the answer.	Write the sum or difference in simplest form.

$$\frac{1}{8} + \frac{3}{8} = \frac{4}{}$$ $$\frac{1}{8} + \frac{3}{8} = \frac{4}{8}$$ $$\frac{4}{8} = \frac{1}{2}$$

Write each sum or difference in simplest form.

1. $\frac{5}{7} - \frac{4}{7} =$ $\frac{3}{10} + \frac{7}{10} =$

2. $\frac{5}{6} + \frac{5}{6} =$ $\frac{2}{15} + \frac{8}{15} =$

3. $\frac{15}{20} - \frac{8}{20} =$ $\frac{10}{11} - \frac{4}{11} =$

4.
$$\begin{array}{r} \frac{4}{9} \\ +\ \frac{8}{9} \\ \hline \end{array} \qquad \begin{array}{r} \frac{3}{5} \\ +\ \frac{4}{5} \\ \hline \end{array} \qquad \begin{array}{r} \frac{5}{6} \\ -\ \frac{1}{6} \\ \hline \end{array}$$

5.
$$\begin{array}{r} \frac{9}{10} \\ -\ \frac{3}{10} \\ \hline \end{array} \qquad \begin{array}{r} \frac{4}{7} \\ +\ \frac{6}{7} \\ \hline \end{array} \qquad \begin{array}{r} \frac{3}{8} \\ -\ \frac{1}{8} \\ \hline \end{array}$$

Adding and Subtracting Mixed Numbers with Like Denominators

To add or subtract mixed numbers whose fractions have the same denominator:

Step 1	Step 2	Step 3
Add or subtract the numerators of the fraction part.	Add or subtract the whole numbers.	Simplify.

Step 1

$$2\frac{7}{9}$$
$$+\,4\frac{8}{9}$$
$$\overline{\quad\frac{15}{9}}$$

Step 2

$$2\frac{7}{9}$$
$$+\,4\frac{8}{9}$$
$$\overline{\;6\frac{15}{9}}$$

Step 3

$$2\frac{7}{9}$$
$$+\,4\frac{8}{9}$$
$$\overline{\;6\frac{15}{9}} =$$
$$7\frac{6}{9} \text{ or } 7\frac{2}{3}$$

Write each sum or difference in simplest form.

1.
$$4\frac{7}{8}$$
$$+\,1\frac{1}{8}$$

$$2\frac{4}{9}$$
$$-\,1\frac{1}{9}$$

$$3\frac{7}{12}$$
$$-\,2\frac{1}{12}$$

2.
$$6\frac{4}{5}$$
$$+\,3\frac{3}{5}$$

$$8\frac{3}{15}$$
$$+\,7\frac{7}{15}$$

$$4\frac{6}{7}$$
$$-\,1\frac{2}{7}$$

3.
$$3\frac{5}{12}$$
$$-\,2$$

$$7\frac{2}{3}$$
$$-\,7$$

$$4\frac{5}{6}$$
$$-\,1\frac{5}{6}$$

RB-904002

You may need to rename a mixed number before you subtract. **Example:** $7\frac{1}{9} - 2\frac{4}{9}$	Subtract, and write the difference in simplest form.
$7\frac{1}{9} = \mathbf{6} + \frac{9}{9} + \frac{1}{9} = 6\frac{10}{9}$ $\qquad -2\frac{4}{9} \qquad\qquad\qquad -2\frac{4}{9}$	$\begin{array}{r} 6\frac{10}{9} \\ -2\frac{4}{9} \\ \hline 4\frac{6}{9} = \mathbf{4\frac{2}{3}} \end{array}$

Write each difference in simplest form.

1.
$$7\frac{4}{9}$$
$$-2\frac{4}{9}$$

$$2\frac{5}{8}$$
$$-\ \frac{7}{8}$$

$$5\frac{1}{6}$$
$$-2\frac{5}{6}$$

2.
$$4\frac{3}{7}$$
$$-1\frac{5}{7}$$

$$6\frac{4}{15}$$
$$-4\frac{7}{15}$$

$$8\frac{2}{5}$$
$$-3\frac{4}{5}$$

3.
$$9$$
$$-3\frac{2}{8}$$

$$6$$
$$-1\frac{1}{2}$$

$$5$$
$$-2\frac{3}{4}$$

4.
$$24$$
$$-17\frac{2}{3}$$

$$20\frac{3}{5}$$
$$-19\frac{4}{5}$$

$$16$$
$$-13\frac{6}{8}$$

Adding and Subtracting Fractions with Unlike Denominators

Write equivalent fractions with the lowest common denominator. Then add or subtract the numerator. Simplify your answer.

$$\frac{5}{6} = \frac{10}{12}$$
$$+\frac{3}{4} = +\frac{9}{12}$$
$$\frac{19}{12} = 1\frac{7}{12}$$

Add or subtract. Write the answer in simplest form.

1. $\frac{3}{5} - \frac{1}{4}$ $\frac{4}{9} + \frac{2}{3}$ $\frac{3}{10} + \frac{3}{4}$

2. $\frac{5}{6} - \frac{1}{7}$ $\frac{2}{3} + \frac{5}{9}$ $\frac{1}{8} + \frac{4}{5}$

3. $\frac{4}{7} + \frac{6}{9}$ $\frac{6}{7} - \frac{2}{5}$ $\frac{10}{15} - \frac{2}{6}$

4. $\frac{4}{8} - \frac{7}{16}$ $\frac{8}{10} - \frac{1}{5}$ $\frac{4}{15} + \frac{6}{10}$

RB-904002

Subtracting with Improper Fractions

Example:

You can also subtract mixed numbers by changing them to improper fractions.

$$4\tfrac{1}{4} = \tfrac{17}{4}$$ ← Subtract the numerators.

$$-1\tfrac{3}{4} = -\tfrac{7}{4}$$ Simplify.

$$\tfrac{10}{4} = 2\tfrac{2}{4} = 2\tfrac{1}{2}$$

Subtract by changing the mixed numbers to improper fractions. Simplify your answer.

1.

$$8\tfrac{1}{5} = \tfrac{41}{5}$$
$$-3\tfrac{4}{5} = -\tfrac{19}{5}$$
$$\tfrac{22}{5} = 4\tfrac{2}{5}$$

$$6\tfrac{1}{8} =$$
$$-1\tfrac{2}{8} =$$

2.

$$5\tfrac{2}{5} =$$
$$-2\tfrac{3}{5} =$$

$$4\tfrac{2}{8} =$$
$$-3\tfrac{6}{8} =$$

3.

$$10\tfrac{3}{8} =$$
$$-6\tfrac{5}{8} =$$

$$6\tfrac{3}{6} =$$
$$-2\tfrac{5}{6} =$$

4.

$$14\tfrac{3}{5} =$$
$$-8\tfrac{4}{5} =$$

$$16\tfrac{6}{8} =$$
$$-9\tfrac{7}{8} =$$

Adding and Subtracting Mixed Numbers with Unlike Denominators

Step 1	**Step 2**	**Step 3**	**Step 4**
Write equivalent fractions with the lowest common denominator.	Add or subtract the numerators of the fractions.	Add or subtract the whole numbers.	Simplify.

$$
\begin{aligned}
4\tfrac{5}{6} &= 4\tfrac{15}{18} \\
-1\tfrac{3}{9} &= -1\tfrac{6}{18}
\end{aligned}
$$

Step 2:
$$
\begin{aligned}
4\tfrac{15}{18} \\
-1\tfrac{6}{18} \\
\hline
\tfrac{9}{18}
\end{aligned}
$$

Step 3:
$$
\begin{aligned}
4\tfrac{15}{18} \\
-1\tfrac{6}{18} \\
\hline
3\tfrac{9}{18}
\end{aligned}
$$

Step 4:
$$
\begin{aligned}
4\tfrac{15}{18} \\
-1\tfrac{6}{18} \\
\hline
3\tfrac{9}{18} \\
= 3\tfrac{1}{2}
\end{aligned}
$$

Add or subtract. Write the answer in simplest form.

1. $8\tfrac{3}{8}$ $-5\tfrac{1}{6}$ $6\tfrac{3}{5}$ $-2\tfrac{1}{4}$ $4\tfrac{1}{2}$ $-2\tfrac{1}{3}$

2. $11\tfrac{4}{5}$ $+24\tfrac{2}{3}$ $6\tfrac{3}{7}$ $+9\tfrac{2}{4}$ $4\tfrac{4}{9}$ $+10\tfrac{3}{4}$

3. $12\tfrac{2}{7}$ $-7\tfrac{1}{3}$ $9\tfrac{8}{15}$ $-6\tfrac{1}{5}$ $18\tfrac{6}{7}$ $-7\tfrac{10}{14}$

RB-904002

Adding and Subtracting Mixed Numbers with Unlike Denominators

Add or subtract. Write the answer in simplest form.

1. $6\frac{1}{4}$ $-4\frac{7}{16}$

$7\frac{1}{7}$ $+3\frac{6}{14}$

$8\frac{1}{3}$ $-2\frac{9}{15}$

2. $9\frac{1}{18}$ $+5\frac{3}{6}$

$3\frac{1}{10}$ $-1\frac{4}{5}$

$5\frac{1}{16}$ $+4\frac{6}{8}$

3. $17\frac{2}{6}$ $-2\frac{9}{18}$

$14\frac{3}{8}$ $+1\frac{8}{16}$

$18\frac{2}{6}$ $-5\frac{9}{15}$

4. $23\frac{1}{10}$ $+11\frac{4}{5}$

$19\frac{2}{4}$ $-14\frac{10}{12}$

$32\frac{7}{16}$ $+20\frac{3}{4}$

5. $26\frac{2}{16}$ $-17\frac{7}{8}$

$28\frac{7}{12}$ $+19\frac{5}{6}$

$13\frac{12}{20}$ $-12\frac{4}{5}$

www.summerbridgeactivities.com   © Rainbow Bridge Publishing

Addition and Subtraction Practice with Magic Squares

When you add the numbers in each row, column, and diagonal of a magic square, the sums are the same. Find the missing numbers in each magic square below. The magic sums are given.

$1\frac{1}{4}$		$2\frac{1}{2}$
	$1\frac{9}{16}$	
	$2\frac{3}{16}$	$1\frac{7}{8}$

The magic sum is $4\frac{11}{16}$.

$\frac{3}{4}$		$1\frac{1}{2}$
	$1\frac{7}{8}$	
$2\frac{1}{4}$		3

The magic sum is $5\frac{5}{8}$.

$2\frac{2}{3}$		$1\frac{1}{3}$
2		$\frac{2}{3}$

The magic sum is 5.

3		$1\frac{1}{2}$
6		$4\frac{1}{2}$

The magic sum is $11\frac{1}{4}$.

© Rainbow Bridge Publishing

RB-904002

Fractions Problem Solving

Use the information in the recipe to solve each problem. Write answers in simplest form.

1. Mrs. Johnson plans to make a batch of trail mix using more raisins than the recipe requires. If she doubles the amount of raisins, how many cups of raisins will she need?

Trail Mix Recipe
$1\frac{1}{4}$ cups sunflower seeds
$1\frac{1}{2}$ cups peanuts
$\frac{3}{4}$ cup candy-coated chocolate
$\frac{5}{8}$ cup raisins
Makes 1 batch.

2. After measuring the amount of peanuts needed to make a batch of trail mix, Mrs. Johnson had $2\frac{1}{2}$ cups of peanuts left over. How many cups of peanuts did she begin with?

3. Ellen Johnson increased the amount of candy-coated chocolate pieces in the recipe to $1\frac{1}{8}$ cups. How many more cups of chocolate pieces did she use than the recipe called for?

4. If none of the measurements are changed, how many cups of trail mix does one batch make after all of the ingredients are combined?

5. The Johnson family made enough trail mix to take on their hike. They hiked $4\frac{3}{8}$ miles to Green River Gulch and then walked another $1\frac{9}{16}$ miles down the riverbank. How far did they hike altogether?

Fractions Problem Solving

1. In a baseball game, the starting pitcher pitched 5 innings. The relief pitcher pitched another $1\frac{2}{3}$ innings before the closing pitcher came in to finish the game.
   a. How many more innings did the starting pitcher pitch than the relief pitcher?

   b. How many innings did the closing pitcher pitch after he finished the ninth inning?

2. In a city baseball league, the Tigers are $1\frac{1}{2}$ games behind the Pirates, and the Pirates are 4 games ahead of the Cubs. How many games separate the Tigers and the Cubs?

   Clue: Draw a diagram.

3. Softball bats are $2\frac{1}{2}$ inches in diameter. If a softball is $3\frac{1}{8}$ inches in diameter, how much wider is the softball than the bat?

4. Suppose $\frac{5}{8}$ of major league baseball fans watch the games on television, and $\frac{1}{3}$ of the fans listen to them on the radio. What fraction shows how many more baseball fans watch television than listen to the radio?

5. Bob spent $\frac{3}{8}$ of his birthday money at a baseball game and $\frac{5}{12}$ on a new bat and glove. What fraction of his birthday money did Bob spend altogether?

    RB-904002

Multiplying Fractions

Multiply $\frac{3}{4} \times \frac{2}{8}$	Step 1 Multiply the numerators. Multiply the denominators. $\frac{3}{4} \times \frac{2}{8} = \frac{3 \times 2}{4 \times 8}$ $= \frac{6}{32}$	Step 2 Write the fraction in simplest form. $\frac{6 \div 2}{32 \div 2} = \frac{3}{16}$

Multiply. Write each fraction in simplest form.

1. $\frac{1}{8} \times \frac{1}{5} =$ $\frac{1}{4} \times \frac{1}{7} =$ $\frac{1}{12} \times \frac{1}{8} =$

2. $\frac{3}{7} \times \frac{4}{5} =$ $\frac{4}{5} \times \frac{6}{8} =$ $\frac{2}{3} \times \frac{4}{7} =$

3. $\frac{5}{6} \times \frac{4}{5} =$ $\frac{2}{3} \times \frac{7}{8} =$ $\frac{7}{9} \times \frac{8}{9} =$

4. $\frac{1}{2} \times \frac{2}{12} =$ $\frac{2}{3} \times \frac{4}{12} =$ $\frac{6}{8} \times \frac{4}{16} =$

5. $\frac{7}{10} \times \frac{3}{5} =$ $\frac{2}{7} \times \frac{10}{14} =$ $\frac{4}{6} \times \frac{12}{18} =$

6. $\frac{12}{16} \times \frac{3}{7} =$ $\frac{6}{12} \times \frac{5}{6} =$ $\frac{2}{4} \times \frac{10}{12} =$

Multiplying Fractions by a Whole Number

Multiply $\frac{2}{3} \times 4$ **Step 1** Write the whole number as a fraction. $\frac{2}{3} \times 4 = \frac{2}{3} \times \frac{4}{1}$	**Step 2** Multiply the numerators. Multiply the denominators. $\frac{2}{3} \times \frac{4}{1} = \frac{2 \times 4}{3 \times 1}$ $= \frac{8}{3}$	**Step 3** Change the answer to a mixed number whose fraction is in simplest form. $\frac{8}{3} = 2\frac{2}{3}$

Multiply. Write each fraction in simplest form.

1. $\frac{1}{15} \times 5 =$ $\qquad$ $\frac{5}{14} \times 7 =$ $\qquad$ $\frac{1}{16} \times 8 =$

2. $\frac{6}{15} \times 4 =$ $\qquad$ $\frac{5}{12} \times 6 =$ $\qquad$ $\frac{3}{16} \times 8 =$

3. $\frac{9}{12} \times 3 =$ $\qquad$ $\frac{4}{18} \times 6 =$ $\qquad$ $\frac{5}{15} \times 10 =$

4. $2 \times \frac{9}{10} =$ $\qquad$ $6 \times \frac{3}{18} =$ $\qquad$ $4 \times \frac{6}{16} =$

5. $3 \times \frac{4}{15} =$ $\qquad$ $5 \times \frac{10}{12} =$ $\qquad$ $5 \times \frac{3}{6} =$

RB-904002

Multiplying Mixed Numbers

Multiply $\frac{3}{4} \times 1\frac{4}{5}$ **Step 1** Write the mixed number as an improper fraction. $\frac{3}{4} \times 1\frac{4}{5} = \frac{3}{4} \times \frac{9}{5}$	**Step 2** Multiply the numerators. Multiply the denominators. $\frac{3}{4} \times \frac{9}{5} = \frac{3 \times 9}{4 \times 5}$ $= \frac{27}{20}$	**Step 3** Change the answer to a mixed number whose fraction is in simplest form. $\frac{27}{20} = 1\frac{7}{20}$

Multiply. Write each fraction in simplest form.

1. $\frac{1}{3} \times 3\frac{1}{4} =$ $\frac{1}{2} \times 2\frac{1}{5} =$ $\frac{2}{4} \times 2\frac{1}{6} =$

2. $\frac{3}{6} \times 4\frac{3}{4} =$ $\frac{4}{8} \times 5\frac{2}{3} =$ $6\frac{1}{3} \times \frac{1}{8} =$

3. $2\frac{3}{4} \times \frac{3}{5} =$ $4\frac{2}{5} \times \frac{3}{4} =$ $1\frac{2}{7} \times \frac{2}{4} =$

4. $\frac{1}{10} \times 5\frac{1}{4} =$ $\frac{1}{5} \times 4\frac{1}{2} =$ $\frac{2}{15} \times 10\frac{2}{4} =$

5. $7\frac{1}{2} \times \frac{1}{12} =$ $3\frac{1}{4} \times \frac{1}{13} =$ $2\frac{3}{4} \times \frac{2}{11} =$

www.summerbridgeactivities.com   © Rainbow Bridge Publishing

Multiplying Mixed Numbers

Multiply $1\frac{2}{3} \times 4\frac{2}{5}$ **Step 1** Write the mixed numbers as improper fractions. $1\frac{2}{3} = \frac{5}{3}$ $4\frac{2}{5} = \frac{22}{5}$	**Step 2** Multiply the numerators. Multiply the denominators. $\frac{5}{3} \times \frac{22}{5} = \frac{5 \times 22}{3 \times 5}$ $= \frac{110}{15}$	**Step 3** Change the answer to a mixed number whose fraction is in simplest form. $\frac{110}{15} = 7\frac{5}{15} = 7\frac{1}{3}$

Multiply. Write each answer as a fraction or a mixed number in simplest form.

1. $3\frac{1}{3} \times 4\frac{1}{40} =$ $\qquad$ $2\frac{1}{5} \times 1\frac{1}{6} =$ $\qquad$ $2\frac{1}{4} \times 2\frac{1}{2} =$

2. $1\frac{1}{6} \times 2\frac{1}{7} =$ $\qquad$ $4\frac{1}{8} \times 1\frac{1}{8} =$ $\qquad$ $3\frac{1}{2} \times 3\frac{3}{4} =$

3. $1\frac{1}{4} \times 3\frac{2}{5} =$ $\qquad$ $2\frac{1}{3} \times 1\frac{6}{8} =$ $\qquad$ $2\frac{4}{5} \times 3\frac{1}{6} =$

4. $3\frac{2}{8} \times 1\frac{1}{2} =$ $\qquad$ $2\frac{3}{7} \times 2\frac{1}{4} =$ $\qquad$ $1\frac{2}{7} \times 2\frac{2}{5} =$

5. $2\frac{3}{5} \times 3\frac{2}{4} =$ $\qquad$ $1\frac{2}{9} \times 1\frac{3}{5} =$ $\qquad$ $1\frac{1}{16} \times 2\frac{1}{4} =$

 RB-904002

Multiplying Mixed Numbers

Multiply $5 \times 6\frac{4}{7}$ **Step 1** Write both numbers as fractions. $5 = \frac{5}{1}$ $6\frac{4}{7} = \frac{46}{7}$ ↑ Remember to write the denominator as 1.	**Step 2** Multiply the numerators. Multiply the denominators. $\frac{5}{1} \times \frac{46}{7} = \frac{5 \times 46}{1 \times 7}$ $= \frac{230}{7}$	**Step 3** Change the fraction answer to a mixed number. Simplify. $\frac{230}{7} =$ $32\frac{6}{7}$ $\begin{array}{r} 32\frac{6}{7} \\ 7\overline{)230} \\ -21 \\ \hline 20 \\ -14 \\ \hline 6 \end{array}$

Multiply. Write each answer as a fraction or a mixed number in simplest form.

1. $6 \times 2\frac{1}{3} =$ $\qquad$ $7 \times 2\frac{1}{5} =$ $\qquad$ $3 \times 2\frac{3}{5} =$

2. $2 \times 1\frac{3}{8} =$ $\qquad$ $5 \times 4\frac{2}{4} =$ $\qquad$ $6 \times 2\frac{4}{5} =$

3. $2\frac{1}{3} \times 3 =$ $\qquad$ $1\frac{1}{8} \times 5 =$ $\qquad$ $1\frac{1}{4} \times 6 =$

4. $3\frac{3}{7} \times 2 =$ $\qquad$ $2\frac{4}{5} \times 3 =$ $\qquad$ $2\frac{3}{4} \times 4 =$

Taking a Fraction of a Number

In mathematics the word **of** means **times**.

Example:

What is $\frac{2}{3}$ of **51**?

$\frac{2}{3} \times 51 = \frac{2}{3} \times \frac{51}{1}$ Turn the whole number into a fraction.

$= \frac{2 \times 51}{3 \times 1}$ Multiply the numerators. Multiply the denominators.

$= \frac{102}{3}$

$= 3\overline{)102}$

$= 34$ So, $\frac{2}{3}$ of **51** is **34**.

Multiply. Write each answer as a fraction or a mixed number in simplest form.

1. $\frac{2}{5}$ of 10 $\qquad$ $\frac{5}{6}$ of 24 $\qquad$ $\frac{4}{5}$ of 60

2. $\frac{7}{10}$ of 80 $\qquad$ $\frac{6}{25}$ of 125 $\qquad$ $\frac{5}{8}$ of 96

3. $\frac{1}{2}$ of 15 $\qquad$ $\frac{2}{3}$ of 32 $\qquad$ $\frac{3}{4}$ of 78

4. Four-sevenths of the students in Mrs. Mason's sixth-grade class are girls. If there are 28 students in Mrs. Mason's class, how many of them are girls? **Think:** What is $\frac{4}{7}$ of 28?

© Rainbow Bridge Publishing RB-904002

Multiplication Practice

Below are the titles of four "BOOKS NEVER WRITTEN." To decode the names of their authors, do the exercises below, and find your answer in the code. Each time the answer appears in the code, write the letter of that exercise above it. Keep working, and you will decode the names of all four authors.

A $\frac{1}{4} \times \frac{8}{9}$ **J** $2\frac{1}{6} \times \frac{8}{9}$ **S** $\frac{2}{3} \times 2\frac{3}{9}$

B $\frac{7}{8} \times \frac{6}{13}$ **K** $3\frac{3}{8} \times \frac{7}{9}$ **T** $1\frac{1}{8} \times \frac{4}{7}$

C $\frac{1}{3} \times \frac{9}{11}$ **L** $7\frac{1}{2} \times 1\frac{3}{8}$ **U** $4 \times 6\frac{1}{9}$

D $\frac{8}{13} \times \frac{2}{7}$ **M** $\frac{5}{9} \times \frac{3}{5}$ **V** $1\frac{12}{13} \times \frac{1}{2}$

E $\frac{2}{3} \times \frac{1}{12}$ **N** $\frac{5}{6} \times \frac{3}{5}$ **W** $\frac{3}{4} \times 4\frac{3}{5}$

F $\frac{10}{13} \times \frac{1}{10}$ **O** $\frac{5}{6} \times \frac{9}{10}$ **X** $1\frac{3}{5} \times 2$

G $1\frac{4}{5} \times \frac{5}{6}$ **P** $\frac{4}{5} \times \frac{5}{11}$ **Y** $3\frac{1}{4} \times \frac{2}{9}$

H $\frac{4}{9} \times 1\frac{3}{4}$ **Q** $\frac{1}{5} \times \frac{10}{11}$ **Z** $\frac{5}{7} \times 3\frac{2}{5}$

I $2\frac{7}{8} \times 1\frac{1}{2}$ **R** $\frac{2}{3} \times \frac{5}{7}$

BOOKS NEVER WRITTEN

We've Got to Stop Meeting Like This   by $\frac{10}{21}$ $\frac{3}{4}$ $\frac{1}{2}$ $\frac{16}{91}$ $\frac{1}{18}$ $\frac{25}{26}$ $\frac{3}{4}$ $\frac{3}{4}$

Scuba Diving Safety   by $4\frac{5}{16}$ $\frac{1}{3}$ $\frac{2}{9}$ $1\frac{5}{9}$ $\frac{7}{9}$ $\frac{2}{9}$ $\frac{10}{21}$ $2\frac{5}{8}$

Honesty Is the Best Policy   by $10\frac{5}{16}$ $\frac{13}{18}$ $10\frac{5}{16}$ $\frac{1}{18}$ $\frac{3}{4}$ $\frac{9}{14}$ $\frac{9}{14}$

Friendly Insects   by $\frac{2}{9}$ $\frac{1}{3}$ $\frac{3}{4}$ $1\frac{5}{9}$ $2\frac{5}{8}$ $\frac{1}{18}$ $\frac{1}{18}$ $\frac{9}{14}$ $\frac{2}{9}$ $\frac{7}{9}$

30

Problem Solving

Solve each problem.
Write answers in simplest terms.

1. If Denise walks at a rate of 4 miles per hour, how far can she walk in $2\frac{3}{4}$ hours?

2. Karen was taking piano lessons. She was required to practice $\frac{3}{4}$ hour each night after dinner. How many minutes is that?

3. Scott is going to plant bushes $3\frac{1}{2}$ feet high along his fence. The fence is $1\frac{1}{2}$ times as high as the bushes. What is the height of the fence?

4. Ms. Reynolds has packed some training manuals for shipment. Each manual weighs $2\frac{1}{2}$ pounds. The total weight of the box is $58\frac{3}{4}$ pounds. About how many manuals are in the box?

5. The cooking instructions for a turkey recommend roasting the turkey at a low temperature for $\frac{3}{4}$ hour for each pound. How long should you cook a $10\frac{1}{2}$ pound turkey?

31

Reciprocals

Two numbers are **reciprocals** when their product is **1**.
$\frac{2}{3}$ and $1\frac{1}{2}$ are reciprocals because

$$1\frac{1}{2} = \frac{3}{2} \text{ and } \frac{2}{3} \times \frac{3}{2} = \frac{6}{6} \text{ or } 1.$$

To find the reciprocal of a fraction, reverse
the numerator and the denominator.

Example: Find the reciprocal of $\frac{1}{8}$.

The reciprocal of $\frac{1}{8}$ is $\frac{8}{1}$, or 8.

Find the reciprocal of 15.

- First write 15 as a fraction. $15 = \frac{15}{1}$
- Then reverse the numerator and
  denominator to find the reciprocal. $\frac{1}{15}$
- Check: $\frac{15}{1} \times \frac{1}{15} = 1$

Find the reciprocal of each number.

1.	$\frac{11}{5}$	$2\frac{1}{4}$	9	$\frac{3}{10}$
2.	$\frac{1}{7}$	$4\frac{5}{8}$	$\frac{15}{11}$	$\frac{1}{6}$
3.	$\frac{3}{4}$	3	$\frac{9}{4}$	$7\frac{5}{8}$
4.	$5\frac{2}{3}$	$\frac{7}{9}$	27	$2\frac{1}{5}$
5.	$\frac{1}{3}$	22	$\frac{10}{7}$	$2\frac{1}{8}$

Dividing by a Fraction

Divide. Write each quotient in simplest form.

1. $\frac{5}{6} \div \frac{5}{9} =$ $\frac{3}{8} \div \frac{3}{4} =$ $\frac{3}{4} \div \frac{5}{2} =$

2. $\frac{5}{8} \div \frac{1}{8} =$ $\frac{4}{7} \div \frac{2}{7} =$ $\frac{5}{8} \div \frac{3}{4} =$

3. $\frac{5}{4} \div \frac{1}{2} =$ $\frac{7}{8} \div \frac{3}{5} =$ $\frac{7}{9} \div \frac{2}{3} =$

4. $\frac{11}{6} \div \frac{5}{2} =$ $\frac{3}{14} \div \frac{6}{7} =$ $\frac{7}{6} \div \frac{7}{8} =$

5. $\frac{14}{3} \div \frac{4}{21} =$ $\frac{9}{10} \div \frac{1}{5} =$ $\frac{7}{8} \div \frac{21}{40} =$

Dividing Fractions and Whole Numbers

When dividing fractions and whole numbers, first rename the whole number as a fraction with a denominator of 1.

Example:

Divide $\frac{4}{5} \div 8$

$$\frac{4}{5} \div 8 = \frac{4}{5} \div \frac{8}{1}$$ Write the whole number as a fraction with a denominator of 1.

$$= \frac{4}{5} \times \frac{1}{8}$$ Multiply $\frac{4}{5}$ by the reciprocal of $\frac{8}{1}$.

$$= \frac{4 \times 1}{5 \times 8}$$

$$= \frac{4}{40}$$

$$= \frac{1}{10}$$ Reduce the answer to lowest terms.

Divide. Write each quotient in simplest form.

1. $6 \div \frac{4}{9} =$ $5 \div \frac{1}{7} =$ $\frac{4}{7} \div 8 =$

2. $\frac{3}{5} \div 4 =$ $\frac{5}{8} \div 5 =$ $\frac{9}{10} \div 4 =$

3. $\frac{9}{4} \div 6 =$ $\frac{5}{3} \div 4 =$ $\frac{4}{3} \div 5 =$

4. $\frac{10}{9} \div 4 =$ $\frac{7}{4} \div 3 =$ $8 \div \frac{2}{3} =$

Dividing Mixed Numbers

To divide mixed numbers, first write each mixed number as a fraction.

$3\frac{4}{5} \div 2\frac{3}{4}$ $= \frac{19}{5} \div \frac{11}{4}$ Write each mixed number as an improper fraction.

$= \frac{19}{5} \times \frac{4}{11}$ Multiply the first fraction by the reciprocal of the second.

$= \frac{19 \times 4}{5 \times 11}$

$= \frac{76}{55}$

$= 1\frac{21}{55}$

Divide. Write each quotient in simplest form.

1. $\quad 11\frac{1}{2} \div 2\frac{7}{8} =$ $\qquad 3\frac{1}{2} \div 2 =$ $\qquad 4\frac{1}{4} \div 3\frac{1}{8} =$

2. $\quad 3\frac{3}{4} \div 5 =$ $\qquad 3\frac{1}{2} \div 1\frac{3}{4} =$ $\qquad 6\frac{1}{3} \div 2 =$

3. $\quad 8 \div 1\frac{1}{5} =$ $\qquad 12\frac{3}{8} \div 2\frac{3}{4} =$ $\qquad 5\frac{3}{5} \div 4\frac{2}{3} =$

4. $\quad 9 \div 2\frac{5}{8} =$ $\qquad 7\frac{1}{2} \div 2\frac{1}{2} =$ $\qquad 1\frac{1}{4} \div 2\frac{1}{2} =$

RB-904002

Solving Equations with Fractions

Solve $n \times 2\frac{2}{5} = \frac{3}{4}$ **Step 1** Rewrite $2\frac{2}{5}$ as an improper fraction. $n \times 2\frac{2}{5} = \frac{3}{4}$ $n \times \frac{12}{5} = \frac{3}{4}$	**Step 2** Multiply both sides of the equation by the reciprocal of $\frac{12}{5}$, which is $\frac{5}{12}$. $n \times \frac{12}{5} \times \frac{5}{12} =$ $\frac{3}{4} \times \frac{5}{12}$ $n \times 1 = \frac{3}{4} \times \frac{5}{12}$	**Step 3** Simplify. $n \times 1 = \frac{3}{4} \times \frac{5}{12}$ $n = \frac{3}{4} \times \frac{5}{12}$ $n = \frac{15}{48}$ $n = \frac{5}{16}$

Solve for n.

1. $n \times \frac{3}{4} = \frac{6}{20}$ $\qquad$ $n \times \frac{3}{8} = \frac{2}{8}$ $\qquad$ $n \times \frac{3}{10} = \frac{2}{3}$

2. $n \times \frac{1}{2} = \frac{1}{2}$ $\qquad$ $n \times \frac{5}{6} = \frac{1}{3}$ $\qquad$ $n \times \frac{3}{6} = 1\frac{1}{8}$

3. $n \times \frac{3}{8} = \frac{1}{8}$ $\qquad$ $n \times 1\frac{1}{3} = 3$ $\qquad$ $n \times 1\frac{1}{2} = 20$

4. $n \times 1\frac{1}{2} = 3\frac{1}{2}$ $\qquad$ $n \times \frac{1}{8} = \frac{2}{3}$ $\qquad$ $n \times \frac{2}{3} = 14$

www.summerbridgeactivities.com

Solving Equations with Fractions

Solve $n \div \frac{3}{4} = \frac{5}{6}$	**Step 2** Multiply both sides of the equation by the reciprocal of $\frac{4}{3}$, which is $\frac{3}{4}$.	**Step 3** Simplify.
Step 1 Multiply n by the reciprocal. $$n \div \frac{3}{4} = \frac{5}{6}$$ $$n \times \frac{4}{3} = \frac{5}{6}$$	$$n \times \frac{4}{3} \times \frac{3}{4} = \frac{5}{6} \times \frac{3}{4}$$ $$n \times 1 = \frac{5}{6} \times \frac{3}{4}$$	$$n \times 1 = \frac{5}{6} \times \frac{3}{4}$$ $$n = \frac{5}{6} \times \frac{3}{4}$$ $$n = \frac{15}{24}$$ $$n = \frac{5}{8}$$

Solve for n.

1. $n \div \frac{1}{2} = \frac{7}{10}$　　　　$n \div \frac{5}{6} = 10$　　　　$n \div \frac{3}{4} = 3\frac{1}{2}$

2. $n \div \frac{2}{9} = \frac{1}{5}$　　　　$n \div \frac{3}{10} = 12$　　　　$n \div \frac{1}{3} = 1\frac{1}{4}$

3. $n \div \frac{1}{12} = \frac{1}{2}$　　　　$n \div \frac{3}{8} = \frac{1}{2}$　　　　$n \div \frac{3}{4} = 16$

4. $n \div 4\frac{2}{3} = 1$　　　　$n \div 2\frac{4}{9} = 6$　　　　$n \div 1\frac{5}{7} = 5$

　　　　RB-904002

Problem Solving

Solve each problem.

1. A box contains 10 ounces of cereal. If one serving is $1\frac{1}{4}$ ounces, how many servings are in the box?

   There are _____ servings in the cereal box.

2. A can of soup contains $22\frac{3}{4}$ ounces. If one can contains $3\frac{1}{2}$ servings of soup, how many ounces are in one serving?

   There are _____ ounces of soup in one serving.

3. Ten melons weigh $17\frac{1}{2}$ pounds. What is the average weight of each melon?

   The average weight of each melon is _____ pounds.

4. Christine bought $\frac{3}{4}$ pound of grapes to put in her sack lunches. If she eats the same amount each day and finishes the grapes in 5 days, how many ounces does she eat each day?

   She eats _____ ounces of grapes each day.

38

Problem Solving

Solve each problem.

1. Mrs. Wilson bought $5\frac{1}{2}$ feet of licorice to share equally with her five children and herself. How many feet of licorice will each person receive? How many inches of licorice will each person receive?

   Each person will receive _____ feet or _____ inches of licorice.

   Think:
   How many inches are in a foot?

2. Mrs. Wilson bought a 35-ounce package of flour. She used $\frac{1}{3}$ of it to bake 5 loaves of bread. How many ounces of flour were in each loaf of bread?

   There are _____ ounces of flour in each loaf of bread.

   Clue:
   Solve a simpler problem first. How much of the flour did she use?

3. Mrs. Wilson bought a $2\frac{3}{4}$ pound roast for their family dinner. A total of 9 people will be at the dinner. How many ounces of roast will each person get if the roast is divided up equally?

   Each person will get _____ ounces of roast.

 RB-904002

Fractions to Decimals

Write $\frac{1}{5}$ as a decimal in tenths.

Rewrite $\frac{1}{5}$ as a fraction with a denominator of 10.

$$\frac{1 \times 2}{5 \times 2} = \frac{2}{10} = .2$$

Write $2\frac{14}{125}$ as a decimal in thousandths.

Rewrite $2\frac{14}{125}$ as a whole number plus a fraction with a denominator of 1,000.

$$2 + \frac{14 \times 8}{125 \times 8} = 2 + \frac{112}{1,000} = 2\frac{112}{1,000} = 2.112$$

Write each fraction or mixed number as a decimal.

1. $\frac{1}{2}$ $\qquad\qquad$ $\frac{2}{5}$ $\qquad\qquad$ $\frac{3}{10}$

2. $\frac{2}{4}$ $\qquad\qquad$ $1\frac{1}{10}$ $\qquad\qquad$ $\frac{9}{25}$

3. $4\frac{7}{20}$ $\qquad\qquad$ $\frac{1}{2}$ $\qquad\qquad$ $2\frac{8}{100}$

4. $\frac{3}{8}$ $\qquad\qquad$ $\frac{1}{5}$ $\qquad\qquad$ $5\frac{12}{25}$

www.summerbridgeactivities.com © Rainbow Bridge Publishing

Decimals to Fractions

Examples:
Write each decimal as a fraction or mixed number in simplest form.

$0.15 = \frac{15}{100}$

Reduce to lowest terms ⟶ $\frac{15}{100} = \frac{3}{20}$

$5.6 = 5\frac{6}{10}$

Reduce to lowest terms ⟶ $5\frac{6}{10} = 5\frac{3}{5}$

Write each decimal as a fraction or mixed number in simplest form.

1.	0.1	2.6	0.4
2.	8.7	0.9	4.8
3.	0.20	0.25	0.55
4.	8.08	0.04	0.01
5.	0.42	1.75	0.488
6.	2.500	0.505	3.404

41

RB-904002

Adding and Subtracting Decimals

Line up the decimal points.
Add or subtract as you would with whole numbers.
Include the decimal point in your answer.

Add.
8.25 + 7.62

$$\begin{array}{r} 8.25 \\ +\ 7.62 \\ \hline 15.87 \end{array}$$

Subtract.
17.05 − 11.51

$$\begin{array}{r} \overset{6\ 10}{1\cancel{7}.\cancel{0}5} \\ -\ 11.51 \\ \hline 5.54 \end{array}$$

Add or subtract.

1.
$$\begin{array}{r} 7.59 \\ +\ 2.09 \\ \hline \end{array}$$
$$\begin{array}{r} \$4.88 \\ +\ 6.76 \\ \hline \end{array}$$
$$\begin{array}{r} \$25.90 \\ +\ 34.80 \\ \hline \end{array}$$

2.
$$\begin{array}{r} 10.42 \\ -\ 6.01 \\ \hline \end{array}$$
$$\begin{array}{r} \$52.99 \\ -\ 25.00 \\ \hline \end{array}$$
$$\begin{array}{r} 18.45 \\ -\ 5.10 \\ \hline \end{array}$$

3.
$$\begin{array}{r} 3.041 \\ 5.226 \\ +\ 0.451 \\ \hline \end{array}$$
$$\begin{array}{r} \$15.08 \\ 46.09 \\ +\ 145.73 \\ \hline \end{array}$$
$$\begin{array}{r} \$35.33 \\ 19.38 \\ +\ 10.94 \\ \hline \end{array}$$

4.
$$\begin{array}{r} \$36.05 \\ -\ 14.99 \\ \hline \end{array}$$
$$\begin{array}{r} 6.08 \\ -\ 4.18 \\ \hline \end{array}$$
$$\begin{array}{r} \$58.00 \\ -\ 42.64 \\ \hline \end{array}$$

www.summerbridgeactivities.com © Rainbow Bridge Publishing

Adding Decimals

Sometimes it helps to write 0s to help you keep track of your place value columns.

Add **152.6 + 0.765**

Step 1
Line up the decimal points. Place a zero where it helps you add.

$$152.\mathbf{600}$$
$$+\ \ 0.765$$

Place a **0** in the hundredths and thousandths place.

Step 2
Add as you would with whole numbers. Write the decimal point in the answer.

$$\overset{1}{}$$
$$152.600$$
$$+\ \ 0.765$$
$$\overline{153.365}$$

↑ **Don't forget.**

Add.

1.

$$\begin{array}{r} 0.9 \\ +\ 0.47 \\ \hline \end{array}$$

$$\begin{array}{r} 6 \\ +\ 7.48 \\ \hline \end{array}$$

$$\begin{array}{r} 8.043 \\ +\ 3.97 \\ \hline \end{array}$$

2.

$$\begin{array}{r} 36.764 \\ +\ 877.3 \\ \hline \end{array}$$

$$\begin{array}{r} 97.4 \\ +\ 73.969 \\ \hline \end{array}$$

$$\begin{array}{r} 53.903 \\ +\ 99.8 \\ \hline \end{array}$$

3.

$$\begin{array}{r} 0.6 \\ 0.47 \\ +\ 0.22 \\ \hline \end{array}$$

$$\begin{array}{r} 24.69 \\ 0.104 \\ +\ 682.62 \\ \hline \end{array}$$

$$\begin{array}{r} 7 \\ 32.08 \\ +\ 456.643 \\ \hline \end{array}$$

4.

$$\begin{array}{r} 6.107 \\ 65.48 \\ +\ 183 \\ \hline \end{array}$$

$$\begin{array}{r} 0.72 \\ 2.1 \\ +\ 135.461 \\ \hline \end{array}$$

$$\begin{array}{r} 0.74 \\ 8 \\ +\ 10.9 \\ \hline \end{array}$$

© Rainbow Bridge Publishing

RB-904002

Subtracting Decimals

Step 1
Line up the decimal points.
Place a zero where it helps
you subtract.

Step 2
Subtract as you would with
whole numbers. Write the
decimal point in the answer.

$$
\begin{array}{r}
48.00 \\
-\ 5.73 \\
\end{array}
$$
← Place a **0** in
the tenths and
hundredths place.

$$
\begin{array}{r}
\overset{9}{\cancel{7}}\ \overset{10}{\cancel{8}}\ \overset{10}{\cancel{0}} \\
4\cancel{8}.\cancel{0}\cancel{0} \\
-\ 5.73 \\
\hline
42.27 \\
\end{array}
$$

Subtract.

1.

$$
\begin{array}{r} 6.2 \\ -\ 0.76 \end{array} \qquad
\begin{array}{r} 7.2 \\ -\ 3.94 \end{array} \qquad
\begin{array}{r} \$4 \\ -\ 1.70 \end{array} \qquad
\begin{array}{r} 7 \\ -\ 2.85 \end{array}
$$

2.

$$
\begin{array}{r} \$4.54 \\ -\ 3 \end{array} \qquad
\begin{array}{r} 28.4 \\ -\ 9.63 \end{array} \qquad
\begin{array}{r} 437.1 \\ -\ 67.34 \end{array} \qquad
\begin{array}{r} 268 \\ -\ 168.94 \end{array}
$$

3.

$$
\begin{array}{r} 20.1 \\ -\ 0.673 \end{array} \qquad
\begin{array}{r} 47.2 \\ -\ 0.499 \end{array} \qquad
\begin{array}{r} \$70.23 \\ -\ 68 \end{array} \qquad
\begin{array}{r} 64.6 \\ -\ 35.072 \end{array}
$$

4.

$$
\begin{array}{r} 167.6 \\ -\ 87.907 \end{array} \qquad
\begin{array}{r} 7.2 \\ -\ 0.093 \end{array} \qquad
\begin{array}{r} 4.5 \\ -\ 2.408 \end{array} \qquad
\begin{array}{r} 278.905 \\ -\ 188 \end{array}
$$

www.summerbridgeactivities.com   © Rainbow Bridge Publishing

Problem Solving

1. An owner of a retail clothing store bought a dress for $36.25 and sold it for $59.99. What was her profit? Hint: A *profit* is how much you make after you take out your expenses.

2. Malcolm spent $48.74 on new speakers and $25.39 on computer games. When he was finished, he had only $0.58 left. How much money did Malcolm have before he went shopping?

3. In the town of Sleepy Oak, the fine for a speeding ticket is $32.65 + s dollars, where s is the miles per hour over the speed limit.

   a. What is the fine for going 38.4 miles per hour in a 25-mile-per-hour school zone? Hint: First find out how many miles over the speed limit 38.4 is.

   > **Clue:**
   > Solve a simpler problem.

   b. Mr. Thomas was fined $50.15 for speeding in the same school zone. How fast was he driving? Hint: First find the difference between Mr. Thomas's fine and the base fine of $32.65.

4. Hailey received some cash for her birthday. She spent $14.48 on a CD and donated $25 to charity. She put half of what was left into her savings account. She has $17.76 left. How much did she receive on her birthday?

   > **Clue:**
   > Work backwards.

© Rainbow Bridge Publishing   RB-904002

Problem Solving

1. To make the swim team, Pedro must swim 400 meters in less than 7 minutes. Pedro swam the first 200 meters in 2.86 minutes. He swam the second 200 meters in 3.95 minutes. What is the total amount of time he took to swim 400 meters? Did Pedro make the team?

2. The school record for the 400-meter track relay was 65.5 seconds. This year's Speedsters would like beat the record. It took them 53.96 seconds to run 300 meters. In how much time must they run the last 100 meters to tie the record?

3. The Whiz Kids ran the 400-meter relay in 47.35 seconds. Their time for the first 300 meters was 35.58 seconds. What was their time for the last 100 meters?

Jamie used her pedometer to keep track of how far she walked every week in July. Use the table she made to solve problems 4–6.

July Walking Distance in Miles	
Week 1	7.94
Week 2	13.7
Week 3	9.3
Week 4	11.25

4. Which two weeks together total about 19 miles?

5. What is the total distance that Jamie walked in July?

6. Jamie walked 21.7 miles during the month of August. How many miles did she walk during July and August combined?

Multiplying Decimals: Placing the Decimal Point

To multiply decimals, multiply the same as you would with whole numbers. Then, count the total number of decimal places to the right of the decimal point in each factor. That is the number of decimal places in the product.

$$0.3 \leftarrow \textbf{1} \text{ decimal places}$$
$$\text{x } 8.\underline{\textbf{72}} \leftarrow \underline{+\textbf{2}} \text{ decimal places}$$
$$2.\textbf{616} \leftarrow \textbf{3} \text{ decimal places}$$

↑
Place decimal point here.

Place the decimal point in each answer.

1.
199.6	19.96	1.996	199.6
x 8	x 8	x 8	x 0.8
15968	15968	15968	15968

2.
300.4	30.04	3.004	300.4
x 6	x 6	x 6	x 0.6
18024	18024	18024	18024

3.
250.2	25.02	2.502	250.2
x 5	x 5	x 5	x 0.5
12510	12510	12510	12510

4.
26.4	42.6	18.7	21.9
x 0.3	x 0.6	x 0.7	x 0.4
792	2556	1309	876

5.
21.7	63.1	36.6	3.41
x 4.2	x 2.2	x 4.7	x 6.2
9114	13882	17202	21142

6.
21.43	18.72	24.062	62.003
x 3.04	x 2.17	x 1.3	x 1.4
651472	406224	312806	868042

47

RB-904002

Multiplying Decimals

Multiply **32 x 0.43**	**Step 2** Count the number of decimal places. Then, put the decimal point in the product.	32 ← **0** decimal places $\times\ 0.43$ ← **2** decimal places 96 $+\ 1280$ 13.76 ← **2** decimal places in all
Step 1 Multiply the factors as if the decimal point weren't there. $\quad\begin{array}{r}32\\ \times\ 0.43\\ \hline 96\\ +\ 1280\\ \hline \textbf{1376}\end{array}$		

Find each product.

1.
$$\begin{array}{r}0.4\\ \times\ 6\\ \hline\end{array}\qquad\begin{array}{r}0.9\\ \times\ 3\\ \hline\end{array}\qquad\begin{array}{r}0.12\\ \times\ 7\\ \hline\end{array}\qquad\begin{array}{r}4.9\\ \times\ 8\\ \hline\end{array}$$

2.
$$\begin{array}{r}4.5\\ \times\ 3\\ \hline\end{array}\qquad\begin{array}{r}2.81\\ \times\ 4\\ \hline\end{array}\qquad\begin{array}{r}1.76\\ \times\ 5\\ \hline\end{array}\qquad\begin{array}{r}3.03\\ \times\ 6\\ \hline\end{array}$$

3.
$$\begin{array}{r}2.8\\ \times\ 34\\ \hline\end{array}\qquad\begin{array}{r}6.2\\ \times\ 13\\ \hline\end{array}\qquad\begin{array}{r}3.7\\ \times\ 65\\ \hline\end{array}\qquad\begin{array}{r}0.17\\ \times\ 14\\ \hline\end{array}$$

4.
$$\begin{array}{r}0.52\\ \times\ 26\\ \hline\end{array}\qquad\begin{array}{r}0.208\\ \times\ 21\\ \hline\end{array}\qquad\begin{array}{r}0.836\\ \times\ 52\\ \hline\end{array}\qquad\begin{array}{r}0.92\\ \times\ 27\\ \hline\end{array}$$

5.
$$\begin{array}{r}9.909\\ \times\ 54\\ \hline\end{array}\qquad\begin{array}{r}302.6\\ \times\ 83\\ \hline\end{array}\qquad\begin{array}{r}3.208\\ \times\ 91\\ \hline\end{array}\qquad\begin{array}{r}5.634\\ \times\ 49\\ \hline\end{array}$$

www.summerbridgeactivities.com © Rainbow Bridge Publishing

Multiplying Decimals

Multiply **1.4 x 0.2**

1.4 ←──	**1** decimal place
x 0.2 ←──	**+ 1** decimal place
0.**28** ←──	**2** decimal places

Multiply.

1.

0.7	0.3	0.54	2.9
x 0.4	x 0.5	x 0.6	x 5.4

2.

8.4	0.7	0.9	0.12
x 0.6	x 0.12	x 0.2	x 0.22

3.

56.1	0.45	0.724	0.46
x 2.1	x 0.9	x 0.6	x 0.87

4.

4.95	0.2	9.12	65.1
x 0.3	x 7.8	x 4.3	x 0.25

5.

3.21	4.7	10.16	24.99
x 0.8	x 12.5	x 2.21	x 0.52

RB-904002

Multiplying Decimals

Multiply **1.05 x 0.03** **Step 1** Multiply as you would with whole numbers. $\overset{1}{1}.05$ x 0.03 **315**	**Step 2** Count the number of decimal places. Then, put the decimal point in the product. Write zeros to show the extra places.	$\overset{1}{1}.05$ ← **2 decimal places** x **0.03** ← **2 decimal places** 0.0315 ← **4 decimal places** ↑ **Add a zero as** **a placeholder.** needed in answer, but only 3 numbers

Multiply.

1.   0.091   0.0072   0.0043
         x 0.02   x   0.07   x   0.9

2.   0.33   0.14   0.305
         x 0.0053   x 0.0048   x 0.008

3.   0.165   9.7   0.025
         x 0.08   x 0.002   x   0.6

4.   0.092   0.125   0.0047
         x 0.086   x .023   x 0.83

5.   0.103   0.017   0.0096
         x 0.005   x 0.17   x   0.37

Multiplying Decimals by 10, 100, or 1,000

To multiply by 10, move the decimal point **one** place to the right.	To multiply by 100, move the decimal point **two** places to the right. Add zeros for place holders.	To multiply by 1,000, move the decimal point **three** places to the right.
0.4	**0.40**	**0.400**
10 x 0.4 = 4	100 x 0.4 = 40	1,000 x 0.4 = 400

Find each product. Use mental math.

1. 10 x 0.06 =   100 x 0.06 =   1,000 x 0.06 =

2. 10 x 4.3 =   100 x 4.3 =   1,000 x 4.3 =

3. 0.653 x 1,000 =   1.09 x 10 =   21.3 x 10 =

4. 1,000 x 0.046 =   0.46 x 1,000 =   0.46 x 100 =

5. 1,000 x 3.9 =   0.0045 x 10 =   100 x 0.03 =

© Rainbow Bridge Publishing

RB-904002

Problem Solving

Mike is in college studying to become a nurse. In many of his laboratory classes, he must measure quantities and record data in his notebooks.

1. Mike performed blood tests using 5 test tubes. Each tube contained 12.73 milliliters (mL) of blood. How much blood did he test?

   He tested _____ mL total.

2. Mike's lab partner was using a mixture of water and iodine in 8 beakers. Each beaker had 7.012 mL of the mixture in it. How much of the mixture did he have altogether?

   He had _____ mL altogether.

3. Mike wrapped a cloth bandage around a patient's arm, turning the bandage 15 times before making it secure. He used 9.12 centimeters (cm) each time he turned the bandage. How long was the bandage he used?

   The bandage was about _____ cm.

4. In chemistry class, Mike took a package of salt and split the contents evenly into 9 experimental groups. Each group weighed 0.07 kilograms (kg). How much salt was in the original package?

   There was _____ kg of salt in the original package.

Problem Solving

Mike is in college studying to become a nurse. In many of his laboratory classes, he must measure quantities and record data in his notebooks.

1. In his dietary nutrition class, Mike studied nutrition labels on food. According to its label, one brand of candy bar contained 12.4 grams of fat. If 1 gram of fat contains 9.4 calories, how many calories from fat are in the candy bar?

   There are _____ calories from fat.

2. In biology, Mike viewed a specimen under a powerful microscope. The specimen was 0.021 cm wide. The microscope magnified the specimen 100 times larger. How wide did the specimen appear when it was viewed under the microscope?

   The specimen appeared to be _____ cm wide under the microscope.

3. The normal temperature for the human body is 98.6 degrees Fahrenheit (F). Mike took the temperature of 5 patients. Three were normal. One had a fever of 100.3° F, and one had a temperature of 100.1° F. What was the total of the patients' temperatures altogether?

   The patients' temperatures were _____° F altogether.

RB-904002

Dividing Decimals by Whole Numbers

Step 1
Place the decimal point in the quotient directly above the decimal point in the dividend.

$$5\overline{)3.25}$$

Step 2
Then, divide as you would with whole numbers.

$$\begin{array}{r} 0.65 \\ 5\overline{)3.25} \\ -30 \\ \hline 25 \\ -25 \\ \hline 0 \end{array}$$

Step 3
Check by multiplying.

$$5\overline{)3.25}^{\,0.65}$$

$$\begin{array}{r} 0.65 \\ \times\ \ 5 \\ \hline 3.25 \end{array}$$

Divide. Check your work.

1. $8\overline{)2.4}$ $8\overline{)0.24}$ $3\overline{)0.69}$

2. $2\overline{)45.4}$ $2\overline{)4.54}$ $7\overline{)\$34.37}$

3. $6\overline{)120.6}$ $6\overline{)12.06}$ $4\overline{)2.44}$

4. $6\overline{)5.88}$ $8\overline{)7.592}$ $5\overline{)\$543.20}$

www.summerbridgeactivities.com   © Rainbow Bridge Publishing

Dividing Decimals: Adding Zeros to the Dividend

Step 1 Divide the tenths.	**Step 2** Write a 0 in the hundredths place	**Step 3** Write another **0** in the thousandths place. Bring down and divide.
$$\begin{array}{r} 0.6 \\ 4\overline{)2.5} \\ -2\,4 \\ \hline 1 \end{array}$$	$$\begin{array}{r} 0.62 \\ 4\overline{)2.50} \\ -24 \\ \hline 10 \\ -8 \\ \hline 2 \end{array}$$ ← Write a zero here. ← Write a zero here. Divide by 4.	$$\begin{array}{r} 0.625 \\ 4\overline{)2.500} \\ -24 \\ \hline 10 \\ -8 \\ \hline 20 \\ -20 \\ \hline 0 \end{array}$$

Divide. Check your work.

1. $5\overline{)2.7}$ $\qquad$ $4\overline{)4.6}$ $\qquad$ $6\overline{)5.7}$

2. $4\overline{)0.31}$ $\qquad$ $5\overline{)8.1}$ $\qquad$ $4\overline{)6.3}$

3. $5\overline{)4.19}$ $\qquad$ $5\overline{)3.74}$ $\qquad$ $4\overline{)53.4}$

4. $18\overline{)9.63}$ $\qquad$ $40\overline{)53.6}$ $\qquad$ $16\overline{)5.2}$

© Rainbow Bridge Publishing RB-904002

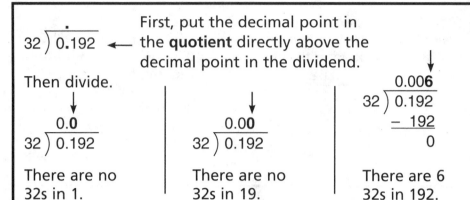

Divide. Check your work.

1. $4\overline{)2.8}$ $7\overline{)0.56}$ $2\overline{)0.018}$

2. $8\overline{)0.52}$ $8\overline{)0.19}$ $5\overline{)0.451}$

3. $24\overline{)0.15}$ $65\overline{)1.95}$ $10\overline{)62.4}$

4. $31\overline{)0.6417}$ $12\overline{)0.42}$ $27\overline{)94.5}$

Dividing by a Decimal

To divide by a decimal number, you must move the decimal to make the **divisor** a whole number. To make the divisor a whole number, multiply both the divisor and dividend by 10, 100, or 1,000.

Divide **5.44 ÷ 1.6**

Step 1
Move the decimal points one place to the right to make the divisor a whole number.

$1.6\overline{)5.44}$ ◄—— Multiply by 10.

Step 2
Place the decimal point in the quotient. Divide as you would with whole numbers.

$$
\begin{array}{r}
3.4 \\
16\overline{)54.4} \\
-48 \\
\hline
64 \\
-64 \\
\hline
0
\end{array}
$$

Divide. Check your work.

1. $0.6\overline{)5.4}$ $0.9\overline{)0.18}$ $1.4\overline{)13.86}$

2. $1.7\overline{)10.54}$ $2.4\overline{)16.8}$ $0.07\overline{)0.035}$

3. $0.005\overline{)0.015}$ $3.2\overline{)13.76}$ $0.63\overline{)0.441}$

4. $0.4\overline{)0.856}$ $2.8\overline{)2.716}$ $0.37\overline{)0.3108}$

        RB-904002

Dividing by a Decimal

Sometimes you may need to add zeros to the dividend.

$$0.65 \overline{)14.3}$$

$$0.\underset{\curvearrowright}{65} \overline{)14.\underset{\curvearrowright}{30}}$$

$$\begin{array}{r} 22 \\ 65 \overline{)1430} \\ -130 \\ \hline 130 \\ -130 \\ \hline 0 \end{array}$$

Divide. Check your work.

1. $0.5 \overline{)255}$ $0.016 \overline{)0.8}$ $0.45 \overline{)9}$

2. $0.4 \overline{)85}$ $0.6 \overline{)261}$ $0.8 \overline{)476}$

3. $0.48 \overline{)16.8}$ $3.5 \overline{)119}$ $0.72 \overline{)3.6}$

4. $.02 \overline{)9.5}$ $0.5 \overline{)23.6}$ $0.51 \overline{)163.2}$

www.summerbridgeactivities.com   © Rainbow Bridge Publishing

Dividing Decimals

To divide by 10, move the decimal point in the dividend **one** place to the left. The result is your quotient.	To divide by 100, move the decimal point in the dividend **two** places to the left. The result is your quotient.	To divide by 1,000, move the decimal point in the dividend **three** places to the left. The result is your quotient.
315.	315.	315.
$315 \div 10 = \mathbf{31.5}$	$315 \div 100 = \mathbf{3.15}$	$315 \div 1,000 = \mathbf{.315}$

Find each quotient. Use mental math.

1. $40.5 \div 100 =$ $2.5 \div 1,000 =$ $70.3 \div 100 =$

2. $983 \div 100 =$ $90.9 \div 100 =$ $4,518 \div 100 =$

3. $88.56 \div 10 =$ $0.009 \div 100 =$ $0.75 \div 1,000 =$

4. $7.03 \div 1,000 =$ $74.41 \div 10 =$ $2.301 \div 100 =$

5. $9.125 \div 10 =$ $6,392 \div 100 =$ $7,452 \div 1,000 =$

© Rainbow Bridge Publishing RB-904002

Writing Fractions as Decimals Review

Another way to write a fraction as a decimal is to divide the numerator by the denominator.

Example: $\frac{5}{8} = 5 \div 8$

$$\begin{array}{r} 0.\mathbf{625} \\ 8 \overline{)\ 5.\mathbf{000}} \leftarrow \\ -48 \\ \hline 20 \\ -16 \\ \hline 40 \\ -40 \\ \hline 0 \end{array}$$

So, $\frac{5}{8} = \mathbf{0.625}$

Write each fraction as a decimal by dividing the numerator by the denominator.

1. $\frac{4}{5}$ $\frac{3}{8}$ $\frac{3}{5}$ $\frac{9}{15}$

2. $\frac{17}{20}$ $\frac{1}{25}$ $\frac{9}{40}$ $\frac{18}{25}$

3. $\frac{111}{200}$ $\frac{5}{16}$ $\frac{45}{200}$ $\frac{8}{25}$

4. $\frac{9}{12}$ $\frac{11}{16}$ $\frac{4}{8}$ $\frac{87}{200}$

www.summerbridgeactivities.com   © Rainbow Bridge Publishing

Dividing Decimals

When finding a unit cost, divide the total cost by the number of units:

$Total Cost ÷ Number of Units = $Unit Cost

Example:

Maria bought a **15**-ounce bag of tortilla chips for **$2.25**. What is the cost per ounce?

Number of Units ⟶ 15)‾2.25‾ 0.15 ← Unit Cost (per ounce)

$$\begin{array}{r} 0.15 \\ 15\overline{)2.25} \\ -15 \\ \hline 75 \\ -75 \\ \hline 0 \end{array}$$

Total Cost

The bag of chips cost $0.15 per ounce.

1. At Orchard Street Market, 4.5 pounds of pears cost $2.97. What is the cost per pound?

2. Mrs. Parks bought 30 ice cream bars for her daughter's class party. She paid $12.60. How much did each ice cream bar cost?

3. Sandy bought a 32.5-ounce package of mixed nuts for $7.15. What was the cost per ounce?

4. A $2.56 can of mix makes 64 cups of lemonade. What is the cost per 8-ounce cup?

5. Whole watermelons are sold for $3.99 each. Sonia bought a watermelon that weighed 21 pounds. What price per pound did she pay?

RB-904002

Dividing Decimals

Did you know that sound energy can be measured in watts? This table shows the energy output of some musical instruments.

Instrument	Energy Output
Piano	.44 watt
Trombone	6.4 watts
Snare Drum	12.3 watts
Human Voice	0.000024 watt

1. How many trombones would it take to produce 1,280 watts of energy?

2. A piano can produce 8 times as much sound energy as a flute. How much energy does a flute produce?

3. A snare drum, a piano, and a trombone are all playing at once.
   a. What is the combined energy output of the instruments?

   b. What is the average energy output of the instruments?

4. How many pianos would it take to produce 4.84 watts of energy?

5. A trombone can produce 80 times as much sound energy as a piccolo. What is the energy output of a piccolo?

Writing Ratios

A **ratio** is a comparison of two numbers. One way to write a ratio is by using a fraction. Roberto's basketball team **won 7** games and **lost 3** games. The ratio of games won to games lost is read **"7 to 3."**

Compare:

games won $\longrightarrow \dfrac{7}{3}$
games lost $\longrightarrow$

Write the ratio as a fraction as shown.

1. 5 cheetahs to 7 tigers $\dfrac{5}{7}$ 20 tulips to 13 roses _____

2. 12 trumpets to 5 violins _____   4 taxis to 9 buses   _____

3. Jill's 23¢ to Bob's 45¢ _____   10 chairs to 3 tables _____

4. 1 meter to 4 meters _____   3 min. to 25 min. _____

Use the table to find each ratio.

Team	Win	Loss
Seattle	49	54
Kansas City	57	47
Oakland	62	42
Chicago	44	60
Texas	56	47

5. Seattle games won to games lost _____

6. Kansas City games won to games lost _____

7. Oakland games lost to games played _____

8. Chicago games lost to games won _____

9. Texas games won to games lost _____

RB-904002

Equal Ratios

Camille reads **2 books** every **3 weeks**. At that rate, how many books will she read in 12 weeks?

Ratio = $\frac{2}{3}$
Denominator is **12**.

Compare:

number of books → $2 = n$ ← books
number of weeks → $3 = 12$ ← weeks

$$\frac{2}{3} = \frac{2 \times 4}{3 \times 4} = \frac{8}{12}$$

So, Camille will read **8 books** in 12 weeks.

Find the missing term.

1. $\dfrac{5}{6} = \dfrac{n}{36}$ $\dfrac{3}{8} = \dfrac{n}{24}$ $\dfrac{5}{7} = \dfrac{n}{42}$

    $n =$ _____ $n =$ _____ $n =$ _____

Use equal ratios to find the value of n.

2. 9 bars of soap for \$3 = n bars of soap for \$9 $n =$ _____

3. 5 points per 2 games = n points per 16 games $n =$ _____

4. 10 tickets per child = n tickets per 5 children $n =$ _____

5. 52 kilometers per hour = n kilometers per 3 hours $n =$ _____

6. 20 people in 4 cars = n people in 8 cars $n =$ _____

7. 40 hours in one week = n hours in 10 weeks $n =$ _____

8. 4 pounds for 16 people = n pounds for 48 people $n =$ _____

Solving Proportions

An equation showing the equality of two ratios, such as $\frac{3}{7} = \frac{9}{21}$, is called a **proportion**.

The cross products in a proportion are always equal.

$$\frac{3}{7} = \frac{9}{21}$$

$$3 \times 21 = 7 \times 9$$

Find the missing term in the proportion

$$\frac{2}{5} = \frac{n}{25}$$

Step 1	**Step 2**	**Step 3**
Identify the terms to be multiplied. These are cross products. $$\frac{2}{5} = \frac{n}{25}$$	Set the cross products equal to each other. $5 \times n = 2 \times 25$	Solve. $5 \times n = 2 \times 25$ $5 \times n = 50$ $n = 50 \div 5$ $n = \mathbf{10}$

Use cross products to find each proportion.

1. $\dfrac{5}{2} = \dfrac{10}{m}$ $\dfrac{3}{a} = \dfrac{9}{3}$ $\dfrac{12}{d} = \dfrac{3}{1}$

2. $\dfrac{p}{15} = \dfrac{6}{5}$ $\dfrac{3}{21} = \dfrac{j}{14}$ $\dfrac{120}{30} = \dfrac{s}{5}$

3. $\dfrac{100}{20} = \dfrac{5}{r}$ $\dfrac{24}{k} = \dfrac{8}{12}$ $\dfrac{g}{15} = \dfrac{8}{5}$

4. $\dfrac{12}{5} = \dfrac{24}{b}$ $\dfrac{27}{18} = \dfrac{6}{m}$ $\dfrac{30}{25} = \dfrac{r}{10}$

65

Percents as Fractions

The number 100 is used in ratios called **percents**.

Per<u>cent</u> means *per <u>100</u>*.

If a grid contains 100 squares, and 75 out of 100 squares are shaded, as a ratio, the shaded part is $\frac{75}{100}$. As a percent, the shaded part is 75%. As a fraction in lowest terms, the shaded part is $\frac{3}{4}$.

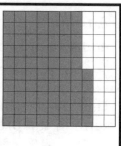

Write each ratio as a percent.

1. $\frac{79}{100}$ $\frac{5}{100}$ $\frac{27}{100}$

2. $\frac{9}{100}$ $\frac{80}{100}$ $\frac{4}{100}$

3. $\frac{86}{100}$ $\frac{150}{100}$ $\frac{99}{100}$

Write each percent as an equivalent ratio with 100 in the denominator and as a fraction in lowest terms.

4.

Percent	25%	3%	50%	33%	65%	56%
Equivalent Ratio	$\frac{25}{100}$	$\frac{3}{100}$				
Fraction in Lowest Terms	$\frac{1}{4}$	$\frac{3}{100}$				

Write each fraction as an equivalent ratio with 100 in the denominator and as a percent.

5.

Fraction	$\frac{3}{20}$	$\frac{1}{10}$	$\frac{3}{5}$	$\frac{9}{10}$	$\frac{9}{12}$	$\frac{4}{40}$
Equivalent Ratio with 100 as Denominator	$\frac{15}{100}$					
Percent	15%					

Percents as Decimals

To change a decimal to a percent, multiply by 100 and write a % sign.

$0.36 \times 100 = 36\%$ $0.04 \times 100 = 4\%$ $0.152 \times 100 = 15.2\%$

To change a percent to a decimal, delete the % sign and divide the number by 100.

$42\% = 0.42$ $9\% = 0.09$ $23.5\% = 0.235$

Write each decimal as a percent.

1.   0.02 =   0.06 =   0.01 =

2.   0.10 =   0.20 =   0.12 =

3.   0.37 =   0.69 =   0.40 =

4.   0.75 =   0.70 =   0.25 =

Write each percent as a decimal.

5.   24% =   65% =   88% =

6.   17% =   9% =   10% =

7.   75% =   20% =   4% =

8.   30% =   90% =   5% =

          RB-904002

Relating Fractions, Decimals, and Percents

Complete the table with equivalent fractions, decimals, and percents. Then match each letter to its answer on the blanks below. Not all of the letters are used.

	Fraction	Decimal	Percent
1.	$\frac{1}{50}$	.02 = S	= Y
2.	= N	= E	3%
3.	= N	0.12	= E
4.	$\frac{3}{8}$	= E	= E
5.	= C	0.35	= U
6.	= R	0.45	= N
7.	= P	= T	50%
8.	$\frac{18}{25}$	= T	= N
9.	= I	= A	90%
10.	= N	1.0	100%

This means "almost perfect."

1	$\frac{9}{10}$	$\frac{3}{25}$	37.5%	0.50	2%

45%	$\frac{9}{10}$	$\frac{3}{100}$	.375

$\frac{1}{2}$	12%	$\frac{9}{20}$	$\frac{7}{20}$	0.03	72%	0.72

© Rainbow Bridge Publishing

Percents: Finding the Percent of a Number

Here are two methods you can use to find the percent of a number.

Multiply by an equivalent fraction.	Multiply by an equivalent decimal.
20% of $130 = 20\% \times 130$ $= \frac{20}{100} \times 130$ $= \frac{1}{5} \times 130$ $= \mathbf{26}$	4% of $25 = 4\% \times 25$ $= 0.04 \times 25$ $\begin{array}{r} 0.04 \\ \underline{\times\ 25} \\ = \mathbf{1.00}\ \text{or}\ \mathbf{1} \end{array}$

Solve using either method.

1. 3% of $10 =$ 4% of $30 =$ 16% of $80 =$

2. 18% of $36 =$ 6% of $80 =$ 9% of $90 =$

3. 8% of $68 =$ 9% of $75 =$ 62% of $62 =$

4. 4% of $400 =$ 3% of $200 =$ 37% of $51 =$

5. 1% of $246 =$ 5% of $286 =$ 60% of $300 =$

RB-904002

Percents: Finding Discounts and Sale Prices

A **discount** is an amount of decrease from a regular price. A discounted price is often called a **sale price**.

Find the discount amount and the sale price for the camera.

$250   40% off

Discount	= regular price x discount rate	Sale Price	= regular price – discount
	= $250 x 40%		= $250 – $100
	= $250 x 0.4 = **$100**		= $150

Complete the table.

	Regular Price	Discount Rate	Discount	Sale Price
1.	$24	40%	$24 x 0.40 = **$9.60**	$24 – $9.60 = **$14.40**
2.	$25	30%	$25 x 0.30 = $____	$25 – $____ = $____
3.	$80	15%		
4.	$220	60%		
5.	$90	55%		
6.	$120	45%		
7.	$1,250	25%		
8.	$198	50%		
9.	$65	15%		
10.	$4	40%		
11.	$80	10%		
12.	$20	35%		

Using What We Know:
Real-Life Problem Solving
Caring for Our Environment

Here are some garbage facts:

- In the United States, 6 out of every 10 aluminum cans are recycled. Each can has a mass, or weight, of about 1.5 grams.
- Each American throws away about 12.2 pounds of plastic packaging each year.
- Every year, each American throws out about 1,200 pounds of organic garbage like potato peels, watermelon rinds, grass clippings, etc. This type of garbage decomposes and can be used to fertilize the soil.
- On average, each American on average produces about 1,600 pounds of garbage each year.

1. What percent of aluminum cans are recycled in the United States?

2. For every 100 cans that are recycled, how many grams of aluminum would there be?

3. A plastic milk jug weighs approximately 0.05 pound. If each American throws away 12.2 pounds of plastic each year in the form of milk jugs, how many milk jugs is this per person?

4. What fraction of each American's yearly garbage is organic waste?

   a. Write this value as a fraction in lowest terms. _____

   b. What decimal is this equivalent to? _____

   c. What percent is this equivalent to? _____

71

RB-904002

Using What We Know:
Real-Life Problem Solving
Caring for Our Environment, continued

Solve each problem. Use the information on page 71 as needed.

5. Some states pay $0.05 per aluminum can that is recycled. If a family of four drinks 24 cans of soda each week (that's one six-pack per person, per week), how much money could the family earn in one year by recycling all of the aluminum cans? Hint: There are 52 weeks in one year.

6. Water is another resource that we need to use wisely and not waste. A bath uses about 20 gallons of water. A short shower uses about 15 gallons of water.

   a. What is the ratio of water used in showers to baths? Write this ratio as a fraction in lowest terms. _____

   b. Fill in the blanks with the correct numbers to complete the sentence.

      For every _____ baths you take, you can take _____ showers and use the same amount of water.

   c. If you took 5 baths per week, how much water would you use in a year if you replaced 2 baths with showers?

      How much water would you save?

      What percent does this savings represent?

The Human Body

Solve each problem. Use the following
information as needed.

Here are some facts about the human body:
- The human body is made of natural elements. Its chemical
  makeup is approximately $\frac{3}{5}$ oxygen, $\frac{1}{4}$ carbon, and $\frac{1}{10}$
  hydrogen. The rest consists of small amounts of various
  other elements.
- Our bodies are made up of about 70% water by volume and
  by weight.
- Although there is a large variation in growth, an average-sized
  sixth grader weighs about 85 pounds. That's his or her mass.
- If we could fill an average-sized sixth grader up with liquid
  like a big container, he or she would hold about 40.4 quarts.
  That's his or her volume.

---

1. What fraction of the body is made up of oxygen or hydrogen?

2. What fraction more of the body is made up of oxygen than
   carbon?

3. What fraction of the body is
   made up of oxygen, carbon, and
   hydrogen together?

4. What fraction of the body is made
   up elements that are not oxygen,
   carbon, or hydrogen?

 RB-904002

The Human Body, continued

Solve each problem. Use the information on page 73 as needed.

5. How many pounds of water mass make up the average-sized sixth grader?

6. How many quarts of water does an average sixth grader's body contain?

7. Red blood cells make up approximately 43% of your blood. Another $\frac{1}{100}$ of your blood is made up of white blood cells. Platelets comprise an additional $\frac{1}{20}$ of your blood. The rest of your blood is made up of plasma. What percentage of your blood is made up of plasma?

8. Blood makes up about 8% of our body weight. How many pounds of a sixth-grader's body mass is made up of blood?

9. The human body gets energy from food. This energy is measured in calories. If a person burns 4.8 calories per minute while walking, how many calories would that person burn during a 20-minute walk?

Answer Pages

Page 3

1. $\frac{1}{8}$ $\frac{1}{4}$ $\frac{4}{8}$ $\frac{7}{8}$

2. $\frac{1}{10}$ $\frac{2}{5}$ $\frac{5}{10}$ $\frac{3}{5}$ $\frac{9}{10}$

3. $\frac{2}{12}$ $\frac{4}{12}$ $\frac{2}{3}$ $\frac{9}{12}$ $\frac{12}{12}$

Page 4

1. $\frac{1}{2}$ $\frac{4}{8}$ $\frac{1}{6}$ $\frac{4}{24}$ $\frac{4}{7}$ $\frac{16}{28}$

2. $\frac{5}{12}$ $\frac{20}{48}$ $\frac{8}{18}$ $\frac{16}{36}$ $\frac{1}{2}$ $\frac{5}{10}$

3. $\frac{1}{8}$ $\frac{4}{32}$ $\frac{5}{6}$ $\frac{20}{24}$ $\frac{16}{18}$ $\frac{24}{27}$

4. $\frac{1}{8}$ $\frac{6}{48}$ $\frac{6}{20}$ $\frac{9}{30}$ $\frac{14}{36}$ $\frac{21}{54}$

5. 3   80

6. 9   60

7. 6   36

8. 66   20

Page 5

1. 7: 1, 7   3: 1, 3
   21: 1, 3, 7, 21   12: 1, 2, 3, 6, 12
   GCF 7   GCF 3

2. 20: 1, 2, 4, 5, 10, 20   6: 1, 2, 3, 6
   32: 1, 2, 4, 8, 16, 32   24: 1, 2, 3, 4, 6, 8, 12, 24
   GCF 4   GCF 6

3. 12: 1, 2, 3, 4, 6, 12   24: 1, 2, 3, 4, 6, 8, 12, 24
   44: 1, 2, 4, 11, 22, 44   36: 1, 2, 3, 4, 6, 9, 12, 18, 36
   GCF 4   GCF 12

4. 9: 1, 3, 9   18: 1, 2, 3, 6, 9, 18
   18: 1, 2, 3, 6, 9, 18   30: 1, 2, 3, 5, 6, 10, 15, 30
   GCF 9   GCF 6

5. 14: 1, 2, 7, 14   15: 1, 3, 5, 15
   35: 1, 5, 7, 35   35: 1, 5, 7, 35
   GCF 7   GCF 5

Page 6

1. $\frac{4}{7}$ $\frac{2}{15}$ $\frac{14}{15}$ $\frac{1}{4}$

2. $\frac{15}{32}$ $\frac{7}{10}$ $\frac{1}{2}$ $\frac{11}{16}$

3. $\frac{1}{5}$ $\frac{15}{16}$ $\frac{3}{5}$ $\frac{1}{5}$

4. $\frac{1}{3}$ $\frac{3}{10}$ $\frac{2}{15}$ $\frac{13}{14}$

Page 7

1. LCM: 10   LCM: 35
2. LCM: 30   LCM: 18
3. LCM: 30   LCM: 36
4. LCM: 40   LCM: 30

Page 8

1. $\frac{25}{30}$ $\frac{12}{30}$ $\frac{36}{45}$ $\frac{15}{45}$

2. $\frac{18}{30}$ $\frac{25}{30}$ $\frac{1}{18}$ $\frac{2}{18}$

3. $\frac{16}{20}$ $\frac{6}{20}$ $\frac{9}{36}$ $\frac{6}{36}$

4. $\frac{24}{56}$ $\frac{21}{56}$ $\frac{11}{22}$ $\frac{8}{22}$

Page 9

1. <   >   >
2. <   <   >
3. >   >   <

4. $\frac{3}{8}$ $\frac{5}{12}$ $\frac{4}{7}$ $\frac{5}{18}$ $\frac{9}{16}$ $\frac{3}{4}$

5. $\frac{9}{14}$ $\frac{5}{7}$ $\frac{3}{4}$ $\frac{3}{4}$ $\frac{4}{5}$ $\frac{17}{20}$

Page 10

1. 4
2. $\frac{1}{2}$ of a mile
3. Billy, by $\frac{3}{10}$
4. $4\frac{1}{4}$ inches longer
5. $1\frac{3}{4}$ hours longer
6. $15\frac{15}{16}$ inches of ribbon

Page 11

1. museums, theme parks, cultural events
2. $\frac{5}{8}$
3. theme parks, cultural events
4. theme parks
5. $\frac{5}{8}$

Page 12

1. $1\frac{1}{3}$ $2\frac{1}{2}$ 5 $1\frac{5}{12}$
2. $3\frac{1}{3}$ 9 $3\frac{4}{13}$ $6\frac{1}{5}$
3. $9\frac{1}{3}$ $6\frac{3}{8}$ $6\frac{2}{3}$ 5
4. 5 $8\frac{1}{2}$ $7\frac{3}{5}$ $5\frac{2}{5}$

Page 13

1. $\frac{26}{3}$ $\frac{27}{5}$ $\frac{5}{2}$
2. $\frac{27}{4}$ $\frac{24}{7}$ $\frac{32}{3}$
3. $\frac{52}{5}$ $\frac{122}{11}$ $\frac{23}{16}$
4. 5   12   8
5. 24   30   60
6. 54   55   26

© Rainbow Bridge Publishing   RB-904002

Answer Pages

Page 14
1. $\frac{1}{7}$ 1
2. $1\frac{2}{3}$ $\frac{2}{3}$
3. $\frac{7}{20}$ $\frac{6}{11}$
4. $1\frac{1}{3}$ $1\frac{2}{5}$ $\frac{2}{3}$
5. $\frac{3}{5}$ $1\frac{3}{7}$ $\frac{1}{4}$

Page 15
1. 6 $1\frac{1}{3}$ $1\frac{1}{2}$
2. $10\frac{2}{5}$ $15\frac{2}{3}$ $3\frac{4}{7}$
3. $1\frac{5}{12}$ $\frac{2}{3}$ 3

Page 16
1. 5 $1\frac{3}{4}$ $2\frac{1}{3}$
2. $2\frac{5}{7}$ $1\frac{4}{5}$ $4\frac{3}{5}$
3. $5\frac{3}{4}$ $4\frac{1}{2}$ $2\frac{1}{4}$
4. $6\frac{1}{3}$ $\frac{4}{5}$ $2\frac{1}{4}$

Page 17
1. $\frac{7}{20}$ $1\frac{1}{9}$ $1\frac{1}{20}$
2. $\frac{29}{42}$ $1\frac{2}{9}$ $\frac{37}{40}$
3. $1\frac{5}{21}$ $\frac{16}{35}$ $\frac{1}{3}$
4. $\frac{1}{16}$ $\frac{3}{5}$ $\frac{13}{15}$

Page 18
1. $4\frac{2}{5}$ $4\frac{7}{8}$
2. $2\frac{4}{5}$ $\frac{1}{2}$
3. $3\frac{3}{4}$ $3\frac{2}{3}$
4. $5\frac{4}{5}$ $6\frac{7}{8}$

Page 19
4. $3\frac{5}{24}$ $4\frac{7}{20}$ $2\frac{1}{6}$
5. $36\frac{7}{15}$ $15\frac{13}{14}$ $15\frac{7}{36}$
6. $4\frac{20}{21}$ $3\frac{1}{3}$ $11\frac{1}{7}$

Page 20
1. $1\frac{13}{16}$ $10\frac{4}{7}$ $5\frac{11}{15}$
2. $14\frac{5}{9}$ $1\frac{3}{10}$ $9\frac{9}{16}$
3. $14\frac{5}{6}$ $15\frac{7}{8}$ $12\frac{11}{15}$
4. $34\frac{9}{10}$ $4\frac{2}{3}$ $53\frac{3}{16}$
5. $8\frac{1}{4}$ $48\frac{5}{12}$ $\frac{4}{5}$

Page 21
1. $\frac{15}{16}$ $2\frac{13}{16}$ $\frac{5}{16}$ $\frac{5}{8}$
2. $3\frac{3}{8}$ $2\frac{5}{8}$ $1\frac{1}{8}$ $\frac{3}{8}$
3. 1 $\frac{1}{3}$ $1\frac{2}{3}$ 3 $2\frac{1}{3}$
4. $6\frac{3}{4}$ $2\frac{1}{4}$ $3\frac{3}{4}$ $5\frac{1}{4}$ $\frac{3}{4}$

Page 22
1. $1\frac{1}{4}$ cups
2. 4 cups
3. $\frac{3}{8}$ cups
4. $4\frac{1}{8}$ cups
5. $5\frac{15}{16}$ miles

Page 23
1. **a.** $3\frac{1}{3}$ innings   **b.** $2\frac{1}{3}$ innings
2. $2\frac{1}{2}$ games
3. $\frac{5}{8}$ inches
4. $\frac{7}{24}$ fans   5. $\frac{19}{24}$

Page 24
1. $\frac{1}{40}$ $\frac{1}{28}$ $\frac{1}{96}$
2. $\frac{12}{35}$ $\frac{3}{5}$ $\frac{8}{21}$
3. $\frac{2}{3}$ $\frac{7}{12}$ $\frac{56}{81}$
4. $\frac{1}{12}$ $\frac{2}{9}$ $\frac{3}{16}$
5. $\frac{21}{50}$ $\frac{10}{49}$ $\frac{4}{9}$
6. $\frac{9}{28}$ $\frac{5}{12}$ $\frac{5}{12}$

Page 25
1. $\frac{1}{3}$ $2\frac{1}{2}$ $\frac{1}{2}$
2. $1\frac{3}{5}$ $2\frac{1}{2}$ $1\frac{1}{2}$
3. $2\frac{1}{4}$ $1\frac{1}{3}$ $3\frac{1}{3}$
4. $1\frac{4}{5}$ 1 $1\frac{1}{2}$
5. $\frac{4}{5}$ $4\frac{1}{6}$ $2\frac{1}{2}$

Page 26
1. $1\frac{1}{12}$ $1\frac{1}{10}$ $1\frac{1}{12}$
2. $2\frac{3}{8}$ $2\frac{5}{6}$ $\frac{19}{24}$
3. $1\frac{13}{20}$ $3\frac{3}{10}$ $\frac{9}{14}$
4. $\frac{21}{40}$ $\frac{9}{10}$ $1\frac{2}{5}$
5. $\frac{5}{8}$ $\frac{1}{4}$ $\frac{1}{2}$

Answer Pages

Page 27

1. $13\frac{5}{12}$ $2\frac{17}{30}$ $5\frac{5}{8}$
2. $2\frac{1}{2}$ $4\frac{41}{64}$ $13\frac{1}{8}$
3. $4\frac{1}{4}$ $4\frac{1}{12}$ $8\frac{13}{15}$
4. $4\frac{7}{8}$ $5\frac{13}{28}$ $3\frac{3}{35}$
5. $9\frac{1}{10}$ $1\frac{43}{45}$ $2\frac{25}{64}$

Page 28

1. 14 $15\frac{2}{5}$ $7\frac{4}{5}$
2. $2\frac{3}{4}$ $22\frac{1}{2}$ $16\frac{4}{5}$
3. 7 $5\frac{5}{8}$ $7\frac{1}{2}$
4. $6\frac{6}{7}$ $8\frac{2}{5}$ 11

Page 29

1. 4 20 48
2. 56 30 60
3. $7\frac{1}{2}$ $21\frac{1}{3}$ $58\frac{1}{2}$
4. 16 girls

Page 30

RON DE VOO
IMA SHARK
LYLE OTT
AMOS KEETAH

A $\frac{2}{9}$ **B** $\frac{21}{52}$ **C** $\frac{3}{11}$ **D** $\frac{16}{91}$
E $\frac{1}{18}$ **F** $\frac{1}{13}$ **G** $1\frac{1}{2}$ **H** $\frac{7}{9}$
I $4\frac{5}{16}$ **J** $1\frac{25}{27}$ **K** $2\frac{5}{8}$ **L** $10\frac{5}{16}$
M $\frac{1}{3}$ **N** $\frac{1}{2}$ **O** $\frac{3}{4}$ **P** $\frac{4}{11}$
Q $\frac{2}{11}$ **R** $\frac{10}{21}$ **S** $1\frac{5}{9}$ **T** $\frac{9}{14}$
U $24\frac{4}{9}$ **V** $\frac{25}{26}$ **W** $3\frac{9}{20}$ **X** $3\frac{1}{5}$
Y $\frac{13}{18}$ **Z** $2\frac{3}{7}$

Page 31

1. 11 miles
2. 45 minutes
3. $5\frac{1}{4}$ feet high
4. about 23
5. $7\frac{7}{8}$ hours

Page 32

1. $\frac{5}{11}$ $\frac{4}{9}$ $\frac{1}{9}$ $3\frac{1}{3}$
2. 7 $\frac{8}{37}$ $\frac{11}{15}$ 6
3. $1\frac{1}{3}$ $\frac{1}{3}$ $\frac{4}{9}$ $\frac{8}{61}$
4. $\frac{3}{17}$ $1\frac{2}{7}$ $\frac{1}{27}$ $\frac{5}{11}$
5. 3 $\frac{1}{22}$ $\frac{7}{10}$ $\frac{8}{17}$

Page 33

1. $1\frac{1}{2}$ $\frac{1}{2}$ $\frac{3}{10}$
2. 5 2 $\frac{5}{6}$
3. $2\frac{1}{2}$ $1\frac{11}{24}$ $1\frac{1}{6}$
4. $\frac{11}{15}$ $\frac{1}{4}$ $1\frac{1}{3}$
5. $24\frac{1}{2}$ $4\frac{1}{2}$ $1\frac{2}{3}$

Page 34

1. $13\frac{1}{2}$ 35 $\frac{1}{14}$
2. $\frac{3}{20}$ $\frac{1}{8}$ $\frac{9}{40}$
3. $\frac{3}{8}$ $\frac{5}{12}$ $\frac{4}{15}$
4. $\frac{5}{18}$ $\frac{7}{12}$ 12

Page 35

1. 4 $1\frac{3}{4}$ $1\frac{9}{25}$
2. $\frac{3}{4}$ 2 $3\frac{1}{6}$
3. $6\frac{2}{3}$ $4\frac{1}{2}$ $1\frac{1}{5}$
4. $3\frac{3}{7}$ 3 $\frac{1}{2}$

Page 36

1. $n = \frac{2}{5}$ $n = \frac{2}{3}$ $n = 2\frac{2}{9}$
2. $n = 1$ $n = \frac{2}{5}$ $n = 2\frac{1}{4}$
3. $n = \frac{1}{3}$ $n = 2\frac{1}{4}$ $n = 13\frac{1}{3}$
4. $n = 2\frac{1}{3}$ $n = 5\frac{1}{3}$ $n = 21$

Page 37

1. $n = \frac{7}{20}$ $n = 8\frac{1}{3}$ $n = 2\frac{5}{8}$
2. $n = \frac{2}{45}$ $n = 3\frac{3}{5}$ $n = \frac{5}{12}$
3. $n = \frac{1}{24}$ $n = \frac{3}{16}$ $n = 12$
4. $n = 4\frac{2}{3}$ $n = 14\frac{2}{3}$ $n = 8\frac{4}{7}$

RB-904002

Answer Pages

Page 38
1. 8 servings
2. $6\frac{1}{2}$ ounces
3. $1\frac{3}{4}$ pounds
4. $2\frac{2}{5}$ ounces

Page 39
1. $\frac{11}{12}$ feet or 11 inches
2. $2\frac{1}{3}$ ounces
3. $4\frac{8}{9}$ ounces

Page 40
1. 0.5   0.4   0.3
2. 0.5   1.1   0.36
3. 4.35   0.5   2.08
4. 0.375   0.2   5.48

Page 41
1. $\frac{1}{10}$ $2\frac{3}{5}$ $\frac{2}{5}$
2. $8\frac{7}{10}$ $\frac{9}{10}$ $4\frac{4}{5}$
3. $\frac{1}{5}$ $\frac{1}{4}$ $\frac{11}{20}$
4. $8\frac{2}{25}$ $\frac{1}{25}$ $\frac{1}{100}$
5. $\frac{21}{50}$ $1\frac{3}{4}$ $\frac{61}{125}$
6. $2\frac{1}{2}$ $\frac{101}{200}$ $3\frac{101}{250}$

Page 42
1. 9.68 $11.64 $60.70
2. 4.41 $27.99   13.35
3. 8.718 $206.90 $65.65
4. $21.06   1.90 $15.36

Page 43
1. 1.37   13.48   12.013
2. 914.064   171.369   153.703
3. 1.29   707.414   495.723
4. 254.587   138.281   19.64

Page 44
1. 5.44   3.26 $2.30   4.15
2. $1.54   18.77   369.76   99.06
3. 19.427   46.701 $2.23   29.528
4. 79.693   7.107   2.092   90.905

Page 45
1. $23.74
2. $74.71
3. **a.** $46.05   **b.** 42.5 mph
4. $75.00

Page 46
1. 6.81 minutes, yes
2. 11.54 seconds
3. 11.77 seconds
4. Weeks 1 and 4
5. 42.19 miles
6. 63.89 miles

Page 47
1. 1,596.8   159.68   15.968   159.68
2. 1,802.4   180.24   18.024   180.24
3. 1,251.0   125.10   12.510   125.10
4. 7.92   25.56   13.09   8.76
5. 91.14   138.82   172.02   21.142
6. 65.1472   40.6224   31.2806   86.8042

Page 48
1. 2.4   2.7   0.84   39.2
2. 13.5   11.24   8.8   18.18
3. 95.2   80.6   240.5   2.38
4. 13.52   4.368   43.472   24.84
5. 535.086   25,115.8   291.928   276.066

Page 49
1. 0.28   0.15   0.324   15.66
2. 5.04   0.084   0.18   0.0264
3. 117.81   0.405   0.4344   0.4002
4. 1.485   1.56   39.216   16.275
5. 2.568   58.75   22.4536   12.9948

Page 50
1. 0.00182   0.000504   0.00387
2. 0.001749   0.000672   0.00244
3. 0.0132   0.0194   0.015
4. 0.007912   0.002875   0.003901
5. 0.000515   0.00289   0.003552

Page 51
1. 0.6   6   60
2. 43   430   4,300
3. 653   10.9   213
4. 46   460   46
5. 3,900   0.045   3

Answer Pages

Page 52
1. 63.65 milliLiters
2. 56.096 milliLiters
3. 136.8 centimeters
4. 0.63 kilograms

Page 53
1. 116.56 calories
2. 2.1 centimeters
3.. 496.2° Fahrenheit

Page 54

1.	0.3	0.03	0.23
2.	22.7	2.27	$4.91
3.	20.1	2.01	0.61
4.	0.98	0.949	$108.64

Page 55

1.	0.54	1.15	0.95
2.	0.0775	1.62	1.575
3.	0.838	0.748	13.35
4.	0.535	1.34	0.325

Page 56

1.	0.7	0.08	0.009
2.	0.065	0.02375	0.0902
3.	0.00625	0.03	6.24
4.	0.0207	0.035	3.5

Page 57

1.	9	0.2	9.9
2.	6.2	7	0.5
3.	3	4.3	0.7
4.	2.14	0.97	0.84

Page 58

1.	510	50	20
2.	212.5	435	595
3.	35	34	5
4.	475	47.2	320

Page 59

1.	0.405	0.0025	0.703
2.	9.83	0.909	45.18
3.	8.856	0.00009	0.00075
4.	0.00703	7.441	0.02301
5.	0.9125	63.92	7.452

Page 60

1.	0.8	0.375	0.6	0.6
2.	0.85	0.04	0.225	0.72
3.	0.555	0.3125	0.225	0.32
4.	0.75	0.6875	0.5	0.435

Page 61
1. $0.66
2. $0.42
3. $0.22
4. $0.04
5. $0.19

Page 62
1. 200 trombones
2. 0.055 watt
3. **a.** 19.14 watts
   b. 6.38 watts
4. 11 pianos
5. 0.08 watt

Page 63
1. $\frac{5}{7}$ $\frac{20}{13}$
2. $\frac{12}{5}$ $\frac{4}{9}$
3. $\frac{23}{45}$ $\frac{10}{3}$
4. $\frac{1}{4}$ $\frac{3}{25}$
5. $\frac{49}{54}$
6. $\frac{57}{47}$
7. $\frac{42}{104}$
8. $\frac{60}{44}$
9. $\frac{56}{47}$

Page 64
1. $n = 30$ $n = 9$ $n = 30$
2. $n = 27$
3. $n = 40$
4. $n = 50$
5. $n = 156$
6. $n = 40$
7. $n = 400$
8. $n = 12$

RB-904002

Answer Pages

Page 65

1. $m = 4$	$a = 1$	$d = 4$
2. $p = 18$	$j = 2$	$s = 20$
3. $r = 1$	$k = 36$	$g = 24$
4. $b = 10$	$m = 4$	$r = 12$

Page 66

1. 79%	5%	27%
2. 9%	80%	4%
3. 86%	150%	99%

4. $\frac{50}{100}$ $\frac{33}{100}$ $\frac{65}{100}$ $\frac{56}{100}$

$\frac{1}{2}$ $\frac{33}{100}$ $\frac{13}{20}$ $\frac{14}{25}$

5. $\frac{10}{100}$ $\frac{60}{100}$ $\frac{90}{100}$ $\frac{75}{100}$ $\frac{10}{100}$

10% 60% 90% 75% 10%

Page 67

1. 2%	6%	1%
2. 10%	20%	12%
3. 37%	69%	40%
4. 75%	70%	25%
5. 0.24	0.65	0.88
6. 0.17	0.09	0.1
7. 0.75	0.2	0.04
8. 0.3	0.9	0.05

Page 68

1. 0.02	2%
2. $\frac{3}{100}$	0.03
3. $\frac{3}{25}$	12%
4. 0.375	37.5%
5. $\frac{7}{20}$	35%
6. $\frac{9}{20}$	45%
7. $\frac{1}{2}$	0.5
8. 0.72	72%
9. $\frac{9}{10}$	0.9
10. ninety-nine percent	

Page 69

1. 0.3	1.2	12.8
2. 6.48	4.8	8.1
3. 5.44	6.75	38.44
4. 16	6	18.87
5. 2.46	14.3	180

Page 70

1. $9.60	$14.40
2. $7.50	$17.50
3. $12.00	$68.00
4. $132.00	$88.00
5. $49.50	$40.50
6. $54.00	$66.00
7. $312.50	$937.50
8. $99.00	$99.00
9. $9.75	$55.25
10. $1.60	$2.40
11. $8.00	$72.00
12. $7.00	$13.00

Page 71

1. 60%
2. 150 grams
3. 244 milk jugs
4. a. $\frac{3}{4}$

b. 0.75

c. 75%

Page 72

5. $62.40
6. a. $\frac{3}{4}$

b. For every **3** baths,
you can take **4** showers.

c. 4680 gallons; 520 gallons; 10%

Page 73

1. $\frac{7}{10}$
2. $\frac{7}{20}$
3. $\frac{19}{20}$
4. $\frac{1}{20}$

Page 74

5. 59.5 pounds
6. 28.28 quarts
7. 51%
8. 6.8 pounds
9. 96 calories

www.summerbridgeactivities.com   © Rainbow Bridge Publishing